welcome to
marriage
oneness

MARRIAGE ONENESS™

FamilyLife Publishing®

5800 Ranch Drive

Little Rock, Arkansas 72223

1-800-FL-TODAY • FamilyLife.com

FLTI, d/b/a FamilyLife®, is a ministry of Campus Crusade for Christ International®

Scripture quotations, unless otherwise indicated, are taken from the New American Standard Bible®, Copyright © 1960, 1962, 1963, 1968, 1971, 1972, 1973, 1975, 1977, 1995 by the Lockman Foundation. Used by permission. (www.Lockman.org)

Scripture quotations marked ASV are taken from the American Standard Version (1901), public domain.

Scripture quotations marked ESV are taken from the Holy Bible, English Standard Version®, Copyright © 2001 by Crossway Bibles, a publishing ministry of Good News Publishers. Used by permission. All rights reserved.

Scripture quotations marked MSG are taken from *The Message,* Copyright © 1993, 1994, 1995, 1996, 2000, 2001, 2002. Used by permission of NavPress Publishing Group.

Scripture quotations marked NET are taken from the NET Bible®, New English Translation. Copyright © 1996–2009 by Biblical Studies Press, L.L.C., and the authors. All rights reserved.

Scripture quotations marked NIV are taken from the Holy Bible, New International Version®. NIV®. Copyright © 1973, 1978, 1984 by Biblica®. All rights reserved worldwide. Used by permission.

Scripture quotations marked TNIV are taken from the Holy Bible, Today's New International Version®. TNIV®. Copyright © 2001, 2005 by Biblica®. Used by permission of Biblica®. All rights reserved worldwide.

ISBN: 978-1-60200-226-5

Design: Brand Navigation, LLC

Photography: Veer, a Corbis Corporation brand (Fancy Photography and Corbis Photography) | Corbis Corporation (Tammy Hanratty) | iStockphoto LR

Printed in the United States of America

First Edition

13 12 11 10 1 2 3 4 5 6 7

FAMILYLIFE®
Help for today. Hope for tomorrow.

Table of Contents

LifeReady and FamilyLife would like to acknowledge the
following three couples for their support, encouragement,
and generosity in making *Marriage Oneness* a reality:

Ed and Judy Ligon

Steve and Christie Bardwell

Tad and Judy Krug

Thank you for helping us build strong, healthy,
and God-honoring marriages.

Every day scores of couples pledge their hearts and lives to each other and then, with a simple "I will," set off into one of life's greatest adventures. No journey on earth promises as much happiness or demands from us as much selflessness as marriage does. It is the ultimate thrill-ride, blending pleasure with pain, satisfaction with sacrifice, conflict with forgiveness, and "love you" with "love me."

Here's what we know: nothing is more fulfilling than a good marriage. Nothing. "Two are better than one," Solomon declared. A good marriage transforms life from black and white into living color.

But marriage is also a dangerous and challenging journey. Pitfalls abound. "I will" can harden into "I won't," and the marriage knot, that's meant to last a lifetime, can quickly loosen.

That's because good marriages *don't just happen*! Only the naive believe that. The truth is, good marriages are all built the same way: with sound wisdom, proven principles, and acquired skills and practices. And these are what *Marriage Oneness* offers.

Marriage Oneness is more than a study or a video experience. It is **success training** for couples who are serious about growing and improving their marriage.

Hopefully that's you! If so, over the next eight *Marriage Oneness* sessions, you will be given insights, interactions, and high-impact applications that will inspire and train you in how to strengthen your marriage, deepen your relationship, and make every day better than the one before.

So get ready to engage in and enjoy this success training. You're in for a great time with some special people. By the time these *Marriage Oneness* sessions are over, along with the discussions and weekly dates that accompany them, you're going to have all the know-how any couple needs to have a successful, satisfying, and long-lasting marriage.

And what could be better than that?

Robert Lewis

Jose & Michelle Alvarez

Jose and Michelle Alvarez met in the summer of 1980 and were married in June 1981. In the first seven years of their marriage, they moved thirty-eight times, which included three foreign countries. Jose formerly played professional baseball for sixteen years and is now on staff with the Fellowship of Christian Athletes Golf Ministry. He serves as the chaplain on the PGA's Nationwide Tour. Michelle is a corporate event planner in Greenville, South Carolina, where they make their home. Together they've been speaking at the FamilyLife Weekend to Remember marriage getaways for fifteen years across the United States. Jose and Michelle have four adult children—Aubriana and Jerome Lopez, married in 2007; Severino (23); and Austin (21).

Tim & Joy Downs

Tim and Joy Downs are graduates of Indiana University. They have been on the staff of Campus Crusade for Christ since 1979 and have spoken at FamilyLife marriage and parenting conferences across the country since 1985. Tim's first book, *Finding Common Ground*, was awarded the Gold Medallion Award in 2000, and he has also authored nine novels. His novel *PlagueMaker* was awarded the Christy Award for best mystery/suspense novel of the year. Together Tim and Joy have co-authored two books on conflict resolution in marriage: *Fight Fair!* and *One of Us Must Be Crazy ... and I'm Pretty Sure It's You.* Tim and Joy live in Cary, North Carolina, and have three grown children.

Bryan & Korie Loritts

Bryan and Korie Loritts are enjoying their second decade of marriage. Together they serve on the FamilyLife Weekend to Remember speaker team, joining in the fight for godly marriages. Bryan is lead pastor at Fellowship Memphis, a multicultural church ministering to the urban Memphis community, an adjunct professor in the Bible and Theological Department of Crichton College, author of *God on Paper,* and an experienced speaker. Korie has worked in various facets of the broadcasting industry and is now a full-time mom to their three children. The Lorittses live in Collierville, Tennessee.

oneness team

Tim & Lea Lundy

Tim and Lea Lundy have been married since 1990. They both grew up in Memphis, Tennessee, and attended the same high school and even the same church. They started dating in college, after which they married and began a life of ministry together. They have served in churches in the Memphis area and then served two years in Bangkok, Thailand. After coming back to the States, Tim attended Dallas Theological Seminary. They then moved to Little Rock, Arkansas, where Tim serves as a teaching pastor at Fellowship Bible Church.

Tim is a graduate of Crichton College in Memphis and Dallas Theological Seminary. He has served in full-time ministry for over twenty years in a number of contexts: college and youth pastor in churches in the Memphis area; chaplain of the International Community School and pastor of the International Community Fellowship in Bangkok, Thailand; and leadership fellow and interim director of Spiritual Formation at the Center for Christian Leadership at DTS.

God has blessed the Lundys with five children—Kate (10), Drew (8), Kent (6), Blake (4), and Jude (3). Four years ago, they adopted two nieces—Lindsey (20) and Mallory (18).

Robert Lewis

Robert Lewis is president and executive producer of LifeReady, an organization that provides high-impact video resources to prepare couples, parents, men, and women to embrace God's best for their marriages, families, and lives.

Robert has authored numerous books and films, including the nationally recognized *Men's Fraternity* series: *Quest for Authentic Manhood, Winning at Work and Home,* and *The Great Adventure.* He also authored *Raising a Modern-Day Knight, The Church of Irresistible Influence, The Life Ready Woman* with Shaunti Feldhahn, and *Culture Shift* with Wayne Cordeiro. His latest release is *Explore,* an easy-to-use, interactive DVD series designed to encourage participants in their faith and in how to share their faith.

Robert also serves on the board of trustees for Leadership Network. In 2001, he was awarded Pastor of the Year by the National Coalition of Men's Ministry headed by Patrick Morley.

Married since 1971, Robert and his wife, Sherard, reside in Little Rock, Arkansas, and have four grown children—Elizabeth, Rebekah, Garrett, and Mason—and two grandchildren.

oneness

the measure of a marriage

I Just Married

II The Oneness Factor

(A) Exploring oneness from Genesis.

"For this reason a man will leave his father and mother and be united to his wife, and they will become one flesh."
—GENESIS 2:24 (NIV)

> *"In order to experience harmony you have to have differences."*
>
> **—Tim Lundy**

(B) Oneness is ___soul-level___ harmony of mind, heart, and will.

(C) Oneness is about closeness, not ___sameness___.

(D) Oneness should ___deepen___ over the life of a marriage.

(E) Oneness doesn't just happen; couples ___make___ it happen.

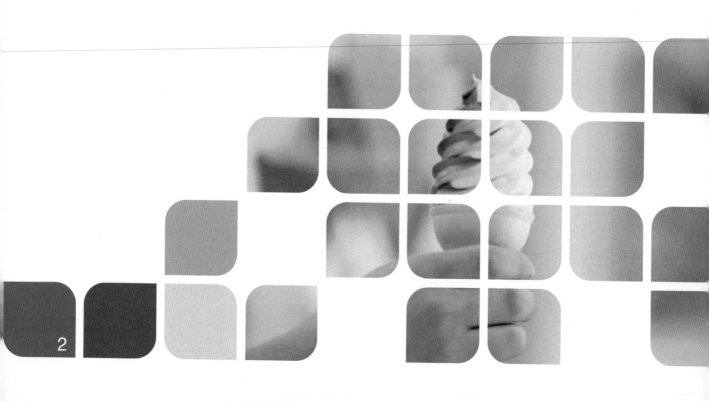

◫ Going Deeper:
The Three Components
of Marriage Oneness

(A) Soul-level harmony of MIND: *common direction*

    1. Do we know where we are going as a couple?

    2. Are we both excited about getting there?

    3. Are we dreaming together?

(B) Soul-level harmony of HEART: *emotional connection*

    1. Can we communicate deeply and openly?

    2. Do we feel connected?

(C) Soul-level harmony of WILL: *mutual commitment*

    1. Are we committed to each other and to our marriage?

    2. Are we willing to pursue new ways to better our marriage?

(D) These three components together

"Finally, all of you, be like-minded, be sympathetic, love one another, be compassionate and humble. Do not repay evil with evil or insult with insult. On the contrary, repay evil with blessing, because to this you were called so that you may inherit a blessing." —1 PETER 3:8-9 (TNIV)

▶ "Be like-minded" ... (common direction)

▶ "Be sympathetic, love one another" ... (emotional connection)

▶ "Repay evil with blessing" ... (mutual commitment)

FAST FACTS:

Willcox Survey: #1 factor for happy wives were those who said that they felt emotionally connected to their husbands.[1]

"Many couples no longer realize that they're hiding a part of their real feelings from each other." [2]

—Paul Tournier

IV What *Marriage Oneness* Offers You as a Couple

(A) This series will give you a hands-on definition of Marriage Oneness you can use in your marriage.

> **Oneness is soul-level harmony of**
> **MIND (common direction),**
> **HEART (emotional connection), and**
> **WILL (mutual commitment)**
> **between a husband and a wife.**

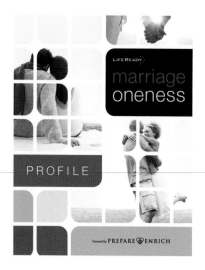

(B) This series will help you to objectively measure the level of oneness currently in your marriage by using the online *Marriage Oneness Profile.*

The *Marriage Oneness Profile* is a vital part of this *Marriage Oneness* series and is included at no additional cost to you. Go to MarriageOnenessProfile.com, and as a husband and wife, you'll each complete the marriage questionnaire. When you've finished, you'll print out a personalized *Marriage Oneness Profile* that compiles your answers and measures both the overall level of oneness presently in your marriage as well as your oneness in a number of specific areas. This *Marriage Oneness Profile* is a highly accurate and proven resource that has helped thousands of couples as they seek to grow closer and stronger in their marriages.

(C)   This series will spotlight and explore seven key oneness areas that are vital to the growth of your marriage:

- ▶ Communication
- ▶ Conflict resolution
- ▶ Money
- ▶ Spiritual beliefs
- ▶ Sexual intimacy
- ▶ Roles and responsibilities
- ▶ Family and friends

(D)   This series will provide a variety of helpful applications and resources for improving your marriage in each of the seven key oneness areas listed above. It will also aid you in applying the lessons to your marriage through:

- ▶ Circle Up discussions
- ▶ OnenessWork exercises

(E)   This series will help make your marriage life ready for a lifetime. It will give you a vision for marriage that works.

> Oneness doesn't just happen; couples make it happen.

Bryan & Korie

Q: If you had to boil it down to one thing, what's the key to "oneness"?

Korie: When we keep Christ at the center of our marriage, everything goes so much better. If we strive to be like Christ, that only makes what we're doing together that much stronger and that much greater.

Bryan: Yeah, I think there's a direct correlation between the good seasons of my faith life and when Korie and I are experiencing oneness. It's uncanny. If I'm yielding to the Spirit of God in my life, exhibiting the fruit of the Spirit, we seem to be able to transcend our circumstances.

circleup ...

(3 couples max)

If you don't know the other couples in your Circle Up group, take a few minutes to introduce yourselves. Then ...

Choose a volunteer to lead your group through the following questions. Please follow these simple small-group discussion guidelines:

- ▶ **Everyone participates.**
- ▶ **No one dominates.**
- ▶ **No one embarrasses his or her spouse.**

1. How was the oneness definition Tim presented in this opening session helpful to you? Explain.

Oneness is soul-level harmony of
MIND (common direction),
HEART (emotional connection), and
WILL (mutual commitment)
between a husband and a wife.

2. Which of the three components of the Marriage Oneness definition is most important to you? Check one and tell why.

_____ Mind (common direction)

_____ Heart (emotional connection)

_____ Will (mutual commitment)

3. What are some of the challenges you face when it comes to experiencing oneness in your marriage? Explain.

4. What questions are you hoping will be answered as you go through this *Marriage Oneness* series?

5. Share one dream you have for your marriage.

What is OnenessWork?

OnenessWork is a special time for you and your spouse to get alone to apply the core concepts of this series to your own marriage. Please don't short-change this time! In order for you to make the most of this *Marriage Oneness* series, be sure to schedule time on your calendar for weekly "dates" where you and your spouse can apply alone the insights you gained from the previous session to your marriage.

Before your date ...

Take the *Marriage Oneness Profile* online. This *Profile* is easy to do and usually takes around 20-25 minutes to complete. It is not a test but a reflection of the oneness you are experiencing in your marriage at this present time. For best results, do not collaborate or discuss your answers before or during this online *Profile*. Take it individually and be as honest as you can. (There'll be plenty of opportunity to talk it over later!)

After you both finish, print out the results (on a color printer if at all possible). You should have a thirteen-page document with your individual responses merged into a *Profile.* The results rate your overall Marriage Oneness as well as your oneness in seven key marriage areas. Individually review the results of your *Profile* before meeting and discussing it with each other. If you have any problems completing the *Profile,* contact your Marriage Oneness leader immediately.

Complete the *Marriage Oneness Profile* as soon as possible in order to have time to discuss your results together before next week's session.

For your opening OnenessWork, you will need at least one to two hours together in a quiet and comfortable setting. Prepare your heart for your date with the following prayer:

> *God, please join us on this Marriage Oneness journey. Help me to learn what I need to in order to be a better and more encouraging partner to my spouse. Help us as a couple to gain new insights into our marriage. Lead us to love better. In Jesus' name. Amen.*

On your date ...

1. Be honest and respectful in your comments as you interact together.

2. ON YOUR OWN: Take a simple personality test. From the opening session you learned that "oneness is about closeness, not sameness." For sure, you and your spouse are different people with different personalities! **So what's your personality type?** Fill out the following chart, checking one adjective per line that you think best describes you. Then total the checks from each column at the bottom. The column with the greatest number of checks represents your basic personality type. Once you have identified which column represents your personality, proceed to number 3 where you will find your personality named and described.

	A	B	C	D	
1	☐ Animated	☐ Adventurous	☐ Analytical	☐ Adaptable	
2	☐ Playful	☐ Persuasive	☐ Persistent	☐ Peaceful	
3	☐ Sociable	☐ Strong-willed	☐ Self-sacrificing	☐ Submissive	
4	☐ Convincing	☐ Competitive	☐ Considerate	☐ Controlled	
5	☐ Refreshing	☐ Resourceful	☐ Respectful	☐ Reserved	
6	☐ Spirited	☐ Self-reliant	☐ Sensitive	☐ Satisfied	
7	☐ Promoter	☐ Positive	☐ Planner	☐ Patient	
8	☐ Spontaneous	☐ Sure	☐ Scheduled	☐ Shy	
9	☐ Optimistic	☐ Outspoken	☐ Orderly	☐ Obliging	
10	☐ Funny	☐ Forceful	☐ Faithful	☐ Friendly	
11	☐ Delightful	☐ Daring	☐ Detailed	☐ Diplomatic	
12	☐ Cheerful	☐ Confident	☐ Cultured	☐ Consistent	
13	☐ Inspiring	☐ Independent	☐ Idealistic	☐ Inoffensive	
14	☐ Demonstrative	☐ Decisive	☐ Deep	☐ Dry humor	
15	☐ Mixes easily	☐ Mover	☐ Musical	☐ Mediator	
16	☐ Talker	☐ Tenacious	☐ Thoughtful	☐ Tolerant	
17	☐ Lively	☐ Leader	☐ Loyal	☐ Listener	
18	☐ Cute	☐ Chief	☐ Chartmaker	☐ Contented	
19	☐ Popular	☐ Productive	☐ Perfectionist	☐ Permissive	
20	☐ Bouncy	☐ Bold	☐ Behaved	☐ Balanced	
21	☐ Brassy	☐ Bossy	☐ Bashful	☐ Blank	
22	☐ Undisciplined	☐ Unsympathetic	☐ Unforgiving	☐ Unenthusiastic	
23	☐ Repetitious	☐ Resistant	☐ Resentful	☐ Reluctant	
24	☐ Forgetful	☐ Frank	☐ Fussy	☐ Fearful	
25	☐ Interrupts	☐ Impatient	☐ Insecure	☐ Indecisive	
26	☐ Unpredictable	☐ Unaffectionate	☐ Unpopular	☐ Uninvolved	
27	☐ Haphazard	☐ Headstrong	☐ Hard-to-please	☐ Hesitant	
28	☐ Permissive	☐ Proud	☐ Pessimistic	☐ Plain	
29	☐ Angered easily	☐ Argumentative	☐ Alienated	☐ Aimless	
30	☐ Naïve	☐ Nervy	☐ Negative attitude	☐ Nonchalant	
31	☐ Wants credit	☐ Workaholic	☐ Withdrawn	☐ Worrier	
32	☐ Talkative	☐ Tactless	☐ Too sensitive	☐ Timid	
33	☐ Disorganized	☐ Domineering	☐ Depressed	☐ Doubtful	
34	☐ Inconsistent	☐ Intolerant	☐ Introvert	☐ Indifferent	
35	☐ Messy	☐ Manipulative	☐ Moody	☐ Mumbles	
36	☐ Show-off	☐ Stubborn	☐ Skeptical	☐ Slow	
37	☐ Loud	☐ Lord over others	☐ Loner	☐ Lazy	
38	☐ Scatterbrained	☐ Short-tempered	☐ Suspicious	☐ Sluggish	
39	☐ Restless	☐ Rash	☐ Revengeful	☐ Reluctant	
40	☐ Changeable	☐ Crafty	☐ Critical	☐ Compromising	
TOTALS					

3. ON YOUR OWN: Circle the letter naming your personality type – A,B,C,D. Then look over the list of strengths and weaknesses that often goes with this personality. Underline the strengths and weaknesses you think best describe you.

A **Popular** **Sanguine**	**B** **Powerful** **Choleric**	**C** **Peaceful** **Phlegmatic**	**D** **Perfect** **Melancholy**
Strengths	**Strengths**	**Strengths**	**Strengths**
Appealing personality	Born leader	Low-key personality	Deep, thoughtful
Talkative, storyteller	Dynamic and active	Easy going, relaxed	Analytical
Life of the party	Goal-oriented	Calm, cool, collected	Serious, purposeful
Good sense of humor	Organizes well	Competent, steady	Perfectionist
Enthusiastic and expressive	Strong-willed	Good under pressure	High standards
Cheerful, bubbling over	Decisive	Avoids conflicts	Detail-conscious
Curious	Not easily discouraged	Patient	Creative
Good on stage	Independent	Well-balanced	Artistic or musical
Lives in the present	Exudes confidence	Consistent life	Philosophical
Volunteers for jobs	Will lead and organize	Quiet but witty	Appreciative of beauty
Changeable disposition	Sees practical solutions	Sympathetic, kind	Orderly, organized
Inspires others to join	Moves quickly to action	All-purpose person	Neat and tidy
Makes friends easily	Delegates work	Easy to get along with	Economical
Thinks up new activities	Insists on results	Inoffensive	Sees the problem
Loves people	Thrives on opposition	Good listener	Sensitive to others
Thrives on compliments	Self-sufficient	Enjoys watching people	Idealistic
Likes spontaneous activities	Stimulates activity	Has many friends	Deep concern for people
Creative and colorful		Has concern	Faithful, devoted
Has energy, charms others		Has administrative ability	Can solve other's problems
		Dry sense of humor	Makes friends cautiously
			Will listen to complaints
			Moved to tears with compassion
Weaknesses	**Weaknesses**	**Weaknesses**	**Weaknesses**
Compulsive talker	Bossy	Indecisive	Remembers the negative
Doesn't follow through	Impatient	Keeps emotions hidden	Moody and depressed
Exaggerates	Quick-tempered	Would rather watch	Off in another world
Dwells on trivia	Can't relax	Hard to get moving	Low self-image
Can't remember names	Enjoys argument	Not goal-oriented	Deep need for approval
Undisciplined	Comes on too strong	Avoids responsibility	Standards too high
Easily distracted	Little need for friends	Quiet will of iron	Hard to please
Scares others off	Inflexible	Too compromising	Prefers analysis to work
Has restless energy	Is not complimentary	Too shy and reticent	Has selective hearing
Egotistical	Dislikes tears, emotion	Self-righteous	Self-centered
Has loud voice and laugh	Tends to use people	Stays uninvolved	Too introspective
Controlled by circumstances	Dominates others	Is not exciting	Guilt feelings
Hates to be alone	Decides for others	Indifferent to plans	Persecution complex
Needs to be center stage	Knows everything	Judges others	Lives through others
Wants to be popular	Is too independent	Sarcastic	Insecure socially
Looks for credit	Can do everything better	Resists change	Withdrawn, remote
Dominates conversation	May make rash decisions	Dampens enthusiasm	Critical of others
Priorities out of order	May be rude, tactless	Fearful, worried	Holds back affection
Easily distracted	Work may become a god		Suspicious of people
Wastes time talking	Demands loyalty		Antagonistic
Interrupts and doesn't listen	May be right but unpopular		Vengeful
Decides by feelings			Full of contradictions

4. TOGETHER: Share your personality types and underlined strengths and weaknesses.

   ▶ What would your spouse add to what you have shared?

   ▶ Where do you see your personality strengths showing up in your marriage?

   ▶ Where do you see your personality weaknesses showing up in your marriage? (Note: Even though we can't change our personality, we **can** minimize our personality weaknesses by being aware of them, and humbly and wisely addressing them. Doing so blesses a marriage.)

5. Now discuss the results of your *Marriage Oneness Profile.*

   ▶ What one insight from the *Profile* was most important to you? Why?

   ▶ What surprises did you find in your *Profile*? Discuss why you were surprised.

   ▶ What is your *Profile* revealing to you, as a couple, about the current state of your marriage? Listen carefully to each other.

   ▶ What other items would you like to discuss from your *Profile* results?

6. Conclude your date by reviewing the Marriage Oneness definition: "Oneness is soul-level harmony of MIND (common direction), HEART (emotional connection), and WILL (mutual commitment) between a husband and wife." Use this definition to discuss the following questions:

   ▶ Do we know where we are going as a couple? (common direction)

   ▶ Do we feel connected to each other? Why or why not? (emotional direction)

   ▶ Are we willing to pursue new ways to better our marriage? (mutual commitment)

7. Keep your *Marriage Oneness Profile* handy. It will be used for engaging the seven Marriage Oneness sessions to come.

communication
and marriage oneness

Two Steps Forward

(A) You received a user-friendly definition of Marriage Oneness.

> "The single biggest problem in communication is the illusion that it is actually taking place."[1]
>
> —**George Bernard Shaw**

Marriage Oneness is soul-level harmony of mind, heart, and will.

1. **MIND:** _____
2. **HEART:** _____
3. **WILL:** _____

Jose & Michelle

Q: What's your best piece of advice on communication?

Michelle: I encourage couples to go deep, to wrestle through issues head-on, to share their feelings and really listen to each other.

It took me a while to understand that this kind of communication was not an indicator that our marriage was bad. I had been seeing our problems as a threat, and I feared we wouldn't be able to solve them.

Jose: Once Michelle knew her heart was safe with me, that no matter what she said I was still going to love her, that's when we really started to communicate.

Michelle: Absolutely.

Jose: Men, make sure your wives know you are committed. Give them total freedom to share their thoughts and feelings without judgment. Freedom and honesty encourage oneness.

(B)   You received valuable and objective feedback on your marriage through the *Marriage Oneness Profile.*

(C)   Some important *Profile* reminders:

    1.   **This *Profile* only measures your marriage as it is right now.**

    2.   **Your Marriage Oneness can always improve.**

(D)   Greater Marriage Oneness requires two key ingredients:

    _____ and _____.

bring it home

Make it a point to take the *Marriage Oneness Profile* each year on or near your wedding anniversary. Let it serve as a "marital checkup." It's a great way to objectively evaluate your marriage.

15

II The Importance of Good Communication in Marriage

(A) We know that communication is vital to a healthy marriage.

(B) Busy schedules, different priorities, and physical exhaustion can get in the way of good communication.

III Sizing Ourselves Up as Communicators

(A) We communicate differently as _____ and _____.

(B) We have been influenced by the way our _____ communicated.

(C)   We each have different communication _____.

1.   Land-the-Plane vs. Enjoy-the-Ride

▶ Land-the-Plane communicators want to find the shortest path to the goal. The destination is the goal.

▶ Enjoy-the-Ride communicators think you might as well relax and enjoy the ride. The trip itself is what it's all about.

2.   Share-Your-Feelings vs. Just-the-Facts

▶ Share-Your-Feelings communicators feel deeply about the things they communicate. Emotions are part of the conversation.

▶ Just-the-Facts communicators set aside emotions for logic, reason, and fact. Emotions interfere with good conversation.

3.   Think-Out-Loud vs. Let's-Take-Turns

▶ Think-Out-Loud communicators ask questions and make comments as soon as the thought occurs—even if the other person happens to be talking at the time. Conversation is a group activity.

▶ Let's-Take-Turns communicators use principles of justice and fair play to govern communication. Conversations are simple: first you talk, and then I talk.

(D)   In good marriages, couples learn how to manage their **communication differences.**

---

bring it home

(circle one)

I think I'm a
Land-the-Plane
Enjoy-the-Ride
communicator.

(circle one)

I think I'm a
Share-Your-Feelings
Just-the-Facts
communicator.

(circle one)

I think I'm a
Think-Out-Loud
Let's-Take-Turns
communicator.

Ⅳ Four Communication Skills That Build Oneness

bring it home

Try stating an "I feel" comment once a day this week. Begin now by jotting down something you want to share with your spouse tonight: I feel …

(A) Open your _____.

"Be kind to one another, tender-hearted … "

—EPHESIANS 4:32

1. Emotional connection should be a top priority for every husband and wife.

2. Share "I feel …" comments.

(B) Become a good _____.

"Everyone should be quick to listen, slow to speak, and slow to become angry." —JAMES 1:19 (NIV)

"He who answers before listening—that is his folly and his shame." —PROVERBS 18:13 (NIV)

How do you become a good listener?

1. **Give focused attention.**
   Don't look up the field; keep your eye on receiving the ball.

2. **Seek understanding.**
   Don't settle for just hearing the words.

3. **Ask clarifying questions.**
   "What I hear you saying is …"

Nothing promotes good communication like good listening.

(C) Learn to speak with _____ and _____.

"Speaking the truth in love ... " —EPHESIANS 4:15

1.   Think, *think,* THINK before you speak.
   Ask yourself, "Is this the best time to say what I'm about to say?"

2.   Use words that encourage and build up.

"Let no unwholesome word proceed from your mouth, but only such a word as is good for edification according to the need of the moment, so that it will give grace to those who hear." —EPHESIANS 4:29

(D) Be aware of your _____ communication.

1.   Communication is more than words.

2.   What your spouse "hears"

▶   _____ words
▶   _____ tone of voice
▶   _____ body language

"You may be saying all the right words, but if you say them the wrong way, you leave the wrong impression."

—Tim Lundy

V Two Sure Ways to Immediately Improve Your Communication

(A) Option one: The 30-minute daily _____.

1. **Establish a regular time to talk at home.**

2. **Turn off all distractions.**

3. **Catch up on each other's lives.**

(B) Option two: An every-week _____ to communicate.

1. **Establish a regular time.**

2. **Focus your conversation on building oneness.**

▶ Common Direction: Where are we going as a couple? (Look forward.)

What's on our calendar this week? This month? This year? Where are we headed? Where do we want to be headed? *Dare to dream together ...*

▶ Emotional Connection: What are we feeling ... *really* feeling? (Look inside.)

Don't try to fix your spouse's feelings. **Just listen.** *I feel ...*

▶ Mutual Commitment: Are we in this together? (Look eye to eye.)

Reaffirm your vows. *I'm committed to you for life ... I love you.*

Bryan & Korie

Q: What have you learned about the art of communication?

Bryan: As speakers, we're always thinking about how to better our communication. But recently I was preparing for a different kind of audience than my normal crowd—and I was really focused on connecting with them—when it hit me: I didn't have that same desire and intention when communicating with Korie.

Korie: We're learning how to be more selfless. Committing to communicate, even on days we're tired, or it's not the right time—to think about the other's needs more than our own.

Bryan: The "communication pyramid" has been revolutionary for us—communicating the *facts,* our *thoughts,* and our *feelings.* A lot of times, Korie needs me to communicate on the feeling level when I feel more comfortable on the other levels. We're both working to improve how we communicate, and we're getting better at it.

VI Communication Is the Life Blood of Oneness

(A)   Remember this week's OnenessWork on communication. You'll need a two-hour date to complete this assignment. If possible, set the time for this date now and arrange for child care, if necessary.

(B)   **Remember: Good communication in marriage takes skill and will.**

circleup ...

(3 couples max)

Choose a volunteer to lead your group through the following questions. Remember your small-group discussion guidelines:

- ▶ **Everyone participates.**
- ▶ **No one dominates.**
- ▶ **No one embarrasses his or her spouse.**

1. What is one thing you appreciate about how your spouse communicates with you?

2. For each pair below, circle the one that best represents your own personal communication style; then share and discuss your answers with the group.

- ▶ Land-the-Plane or Enjoy-the-Ride
- ▶ Share-Your-Feelings or Just-the-Facts
- ▶ Think-Out-Loud or Let's-Take-Turns

3. Which of the four communication skills Tim addressed in this session do you feel you most need to work on? Choose one and explain why.

   ▶ Open my heart.
   ▶ Become a good listener.
   ▶ Speak with more honesty and/or compassion.
   ▶ Be aware of my nonverbal communication.

4. Which would work best for your marriage: A 30-minute daily check-in or a weekly date to communicate? Why?

5. What is your biggest "takeaway" from this session on communication? Explain.

Onenesswork

For your OnenessWork this week, you'll need two hours in a quiet and comfortable setting. In advance of your date, you'll need to think over the following questions in order to make the most of your interaction time. (Use the space below each question to record any thoughts you have **beforehand** and any special insights you receive from your spouse during your discussion.) Prepare your heart for your date with the following prayer:

Lord, use this date to help me gain new insights into my marriage and learn new things about my spouse. Help us to grow closer together. In Jesus' name. Amen.

On your date ...

Commit to strive for better understanding. Stay positive. Start by saying, "I want to hear and understand you, and for you to hear and understand me."

Then take turns asking each other the following questions:

1. What do our results in the Communication section of our *Marriage Oneness Profile* say about our communication right now?

   I think they say:

   My spouse's thoughts:

2. Which **one** of the "discussion items" listed on our *Marriage Oneness Profile*'s Communication page would you like to talk about? Tell me why you chose that one.

I'd like to discuss:

Because:

My spouse's choice:

Because:

3. Tell me one or two practical things I could do to better communicate with you in the day-to-day of our marriage. How would it help you? How would it make you feel?

It would help me if my spouse would:

1.

2.

Those two things would help me by:

They would make me feel:

It would help my spouse if I:

1.

2.

Those two things would help my spouse by:

It would make my spouse feel:

4. In his book *The Five Love Languages,*[4] Dr. Gary Chapman describes five specific ways we love and emotionally connect. (Remember, emotional connection is a key component of Marriage Oneness.) Let's read together the descriptions of the five love languages and then discuss which one makes each of us feel most loved.

<u>Words of Affirmation</u> = I feel most loved when I receive from you compliments, praise, and words of endearment that build me up, cheer me up, and lift me up.

<u>Quality Time</u> = I feel most loved when you make time to give me individual and focused attention to talk, engage, and enjoy life together.

<u>Receiving Gifts</u> = I feel most loved when you give me big or small gifts that communicate how much you value me and symbolize how special I am to you.

<u>Acts of Service</u> = I feel most loved when you do specific tasks that serve and value me.

<u>Physical Touch</u> = I feel most loved when you give me specific kinds of physical touch (holding hands, hugs, kisses, back rubs, cuddling, sex, etc.).

My primary love language is:

Two practical ways my spouse can speak this love language to me in our marriage. (Be specific.)

1.

2.

My spouse's primary love language is:

Two practical ways I can speak this love language to my spouse in our marriage. (Be specific.)

1.

2.

5. In last week's session, Tim pointed out that communication is vital to finding common direction together (a key component to Marriage Oneness). That said, what dreams do you have for our marriage? Be specific and tell me why each dream is important to you.

   My dreams:

   My spouse's dreams:

6. How can we mold our individual dreams into a common direction for our marriage?

7. What is a possible next step we could take together to further improve our Marriage Oneness in this important area of communication? *(Having trouble answering this one? Some suggestions can be found on page 126.)*

Conclude your date by recording your next-step answer on the **Next Steps Planner** on page 127. (Note: From this point on, you'll be asked to select a next step after each session. This is very important. The **Next Steps Planner** will be used to complete this *Marriage Oneness* series.)

successstory

communication

**Mike & Alison
Fendley**

Friends have a tough time believing that Mike and Alison Fendley, now marriage counselors and teachers, were ever truly miserable communicators. But in the early years of their union, Mike often shut Alison down when she wanted to talk about anything beyond the purely functional and day-to-day. And Alison was frustrated that he never wanted to discuss anything—*"and I mean anything"*—on an intimate level.

"By and large," Alison says, "almost every answer I got from him was 'I don't care.' Even on easy subjects—where to eat dinner, what clothes he liked—he always answered the same. And getting to something deeper? Forget it."

"But Alison kept encouraging me to dig deeper," Mike says, "to recognize how I really felt about issues and choices." Over time, they discovered that Mike's past was keeping him from his future. "Basically, I was suppressing my personal feelings because I was afraid she'd reject me," he says. "It was safer to just be 'neutral.' I did care; I just didn't want to risk it."

The Fendleys smile and shake their heads, remembering those early years. They've come a long way. "But the first thing we had to do," Mike says, "was figure out what we wanted. Alison wanted a marriage with open and honest communication. On paper, I did too.

As we worked through our issues, I found I really wanted it in my heart as well. It wasn't easy. It wasn't natural. But the work was worth it."

"We began to share everything," Alison says, "dreams, fears, desires ... but we had to get there with baby steps."

And when she says "baby steps," she means it. Asked for an example, they point to "food preferences." They took a ball and named a food group. Alison named a favorite food in that group and then handed the ball to Mike for him to do the same—"I don't care" wasn't an acceptable response. "It seems silly now," Mike says. "But that's really where I was. We had to start at the beginning. I had to learn what communication really was."

"It worked," Alison says with a contented smile. "We kept going a little wider, a little deeper, and after a while, found we were able to discuss things most couples shied away from—parenting style, in-law issues, financial goals, sexual pleasure, whatever!"

The Fendleys point to praying together for healthy communication and studying the Bible for wise counsel as breakthroughs on this front. They also took classes, read books on the subject, and asked for advice from older couples. Through much prayer— and their willingness to change—they began to experience the joy of open, supportive communication.

But children added new complications. "We worked through them by regularly scheduling time alone. We knew our marriage needed nurturing as clearly as our child did," Alison says. For the Fendleys, it took one date a month, two getaway weekends a year, and one five-day trip every other year to give them the alone time and attention they both needed. They marked those times on the calendar and didn't let anything dissuade them from keeping the dates. "We realized that to be the best *parents* we could be," Mike says, "we first had to become the best *husband and wife* that we could be."

Years later, Alison says, "The Lord is still revealing to us our need to take our transparency to the next level, but we both feel understood, loved. We know we can discuss any issue without personal attack or fear of rejection."

"Listen," Mike says, "we also know what it is to struggle with this. That's because we've lived it. The key is to remind yourself that your spouse is not your enemy and embrace the willingness to be changed. Pray about it. With God's guidance, you can stand amazed at the transformation that awaits you both. We did. You can too."

suggestedresources

Looking for more information on the subject of communication?

The Five Love Languages
by Gary Chapman
Do you know your spouse's love language—and how to speak it? If not, he or she may not know you're expressing love at all. Could it be words of affirmation? Acts of service? Gift-giving? Uncover how your spouse speaks L-O-V-E … and you may even feel more truly loved in return.

Wired That Way
by Marita Littauer with Florence Littauer
Are you frustrated in your relationships? Through our Comprehensive Personality Plan, learn your personality type and how you're wired. You'll be ready to discover 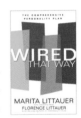 how to maximize your strengths while minimizing your weaknesses. Then, you'll learn how to quickly pick up cues about the personality of others from their body language … and improve seemingly incompatible relationships with friends, family, and co-workers.

**FamilyLife's Weekend to Remember®
Marriage Getaway**
 Life has a way of overwhelming a marriage. Before you know it, checking your e-mail is more important than carving out a date night. FamilyLife's Weekend to Remember marriage getaway is your chance to make a change. Rediscover each other—and find more intimacy in your life together.

Go to FamilyLife.com/weekend to learn more about this weekend getaway.

conflict resolution
and marriage oneness

When Worlds Collide

(A)   Every couple has _Conflict_.

(B)   Every conflict in marriage offers a new oneness opportunity.

1.   Conflict is the fire that forges two " _Me's_ " into one " _We_ ."

2.   Resolved conflict leads to greater soul-level harmony.

▶   Clearer direction
▶   Stronger emotional connection
▶   Deeper commitment

Tim & Joy

Q: What big things have you learned about conflict?

Tim: Everyone has conflict. We've not only had fights on the way to a marriage conference; we've had fights on the way to *speak* at a marriage conference. But conflict *resolution* can be a part of any marriage too.

Joy: Conflict isn't as private as we'd like to think. We've discovered that conflict has a ripple effect on our children, our friends, and the people we work with. It's not just about us.

Tim: And our Creator is always present. There've been times when we've pulled up an empty chair and placed it in front of us as a reminder of God's presence. This has a powerful effect on how we address each other, especially when there's something that's not right between us.

II Why Are Marriage Conflicts So Hard to Resolve?

(A)   We lack basic conflict-resolution skills.

1.   **Wrong timing:** *Never address tough issues when you're stressed or upset.*

2.   **Wrong emotion:** *Beware of anger, the "emotional alcohol."*

3.   **Wrong methods:** *Blame, shame, and defensiveness won't ever bring you closer to oneness.*

(B)   We lack personal objectivity.

"The heart is more deceitful than all else and is desperately sick; who can understand it?" —JEREMIAH 17:9

"Why do you look at the speck that is in your brother's eye, but do not notice the log that is in your own eye?" —MATTHEW 7:3

(C)   We choose the wrong approach.

1.   **The win-at-all-costs approach**

2.   **The withdraw-and-smolder approach**

3.   **The give-in-and-die-a-little approach**

> *"[John] Gottman found that all couples—those who are happily married into their rocking-chair years and those who divorce before their fifth anniversary—disagree more or less the same amount. He found that they all argue about the same subjects—money, kids, time, and sex chiefly among them … What distinguishes satisfied couples from the miserable ones, he found, was how creatively and constructively they managed those differences."* [2]
>
> **—Ellen McCarthy**

III A Better Approach to Resolving Conflict

"For, he that would love life, and see good days, let him refrain his tongue from evil, and his lips that they speak no guile: And let him turn away from evil, and do good; let him seek peace and pursue it." —1 PETER 3:10-11 (ASV)

(A) You must learn to __refrain__ your tongue.

(B) You must learn the __skill__ of peacemaking.

IV The Seven Habits of Highly Effective Couples in Resolving Conflict

(A) Focus on _one issue_, not many issues.

(B) Watch your anger level. If you get off to a bad start, call a
" _do-over_ ."

"A hot-tempered man stirs up strife, but the slow to anger calms a dispute." —PROVERBS 15:18

(C) Practice give-and-take communication with a focus on listening and learning. True understanding is *the* essential ingredient to conflict resolution.

"Let [everyone] be quick to hear, slow to speak, slow to anger." —JAMES 1:19 (ESV)

(D) Attack the _problem_, not the person.

(E) Learn to ask for and give forgiveness.

(F) Seek a resolution _both_ of you can live with.

(G) Always keep your eye on the prize: greater oneness.

bring it home

Get comfortable with these four statements:

▶ "I was wrong."
▶ "I'm sorry."
▶ "Will you forgive me?"
▶ "I forgive you."

V   What to Do If You Get Stuck in Conflict

(A)   Do not let unresolved conflict poison your marriage relationship.

"Be angry and yet do not sin; do not let the sun go down on your anger." —EPHESIANS 4:26

(B)   Together, seek outside help to resolve your conflict.

"Where there is no guidance the people fall, but in abundance of counselors there is victory." —PROVERBS 11:14

Jose & Michelle

Q: What have you learned about resolving conflict?

Jose: I had to begin with understanding my personality in comparison to Michelle's. I'm an outgoing, high-energy, impulsive person; Michelle is quiet, logical, reserved. It helped me to understand that she likes to think through and process a problem—and not always with me or at the same time. She was uniquely made by God, wired this way to help me, and I was wired this way to help her, so it's not about doing it the same way, but more about moving toward each other in the effort.

Michelle: I grew up in a home filled with conflict, so when we encountered it early on, I tried to avoid it. But I later realized that conflict is just two people learning to work through issues in life.

VI Resolving Conflict and Marriage Oneness Go Hand in Hand

(A) When you fight (and you will), fight smart!

(B) Resolving conflict is hard-won oneness.

circleup ...

(3 couples max)

Choose a volunteer to lead your group through the following questions and discussion. Remember the Golden Rule of small-group interaction:

- ▶ **Everyone participates.**
- ▶ **No one dominates.**
- ▶ **No one embarrasses his or her spouse.**

1. What is one thing your spouse does well when it comes to handling conflict in your marriage? Explain.

2. What tends to be your natural response when conflict breaks out between you and your spouse? How does your natural response to conflict impact your marriage and conflict resolution?

3. Which one of the seven habits of conflict resolution would help you the most in your marriage. Why?

4. Which one of the seven habits of conflict resolution would be the most difficult for you to apply? Why?

5. What one thing impacted you the most in this session? Explain.

Onenesswork

This week's OnenessWork is to help you better understand and address conflict in your marriage. Use this time to talk and think through better ways to address the issues that trouble you.

For this assignment you'll need one to two hours in a quiet and comfortable setting. Remember, every marriage has conflict. Good marriages, however, learn to control their conflict with:

- ▶ proven conflict-resolution skills
- ▶ mutual understanding
- ▶ win-win attitudes

Let this date be a positive step for you both in that direction.

On your date ...

1. TOGETHER: Begin your conflict discussion with one of you reading aloud the following passage from Ephesians. These are your conversational guidelines for this time together.

"Let no unwholesome word proceed from your mouth, but only such a word as is good for edification according to the need of the moment, so that it will give grace to those who hear ... Let all bitterness and wrath and anger and clamor and slander be put away from you, along with all malice. Be kind to one another, tender-hearted, forgiving each other, just as God in Christ also has forgiven you."
—EPHESIANS 4:29, 31-32

Commit to each other to honor God's Word in your discussion. You may want to begin your date by **reading together** the following prayer:

Heavenly Father, help us to grow closer together. Help us to hear each other and learn from each other. In Jesus' name. Amen.

2. ON YOUR OWN: Take a moment to answer the following question:

What **two** conflict issues from the following list cause the *most* trouble in your marriage? Mark the top stressor with "1" and the second next highest stressor with "2." (And yes, you should stop there for now.) Be aware that this might be the very first time you've dared to address these conflicts openly—they might be creating silent or indirect conflict rather than verbal or direct conflict. Be brave and share your heart.

I THINK OUR TWO TOP CONFLICT ISSUES ARE:

_____ Housework/dividing chores

_____ Unmet expectations—specifically: _____

_____ Bad habits—specifically: _____

_____ Choice of friends

_____ Lack of time together

_____ Alcohol abuse

_____ In-law relationships

_____ Control or seeking to control

_____ Lack of respect, criticizing, shaming

_____ Religion and/or spiritual beliefs

_____ Parenting (methods, style, discipline strategy)

_____ Money (budgets, spending habits, saving)

_____ Addiction

_____ Recreation (or lack of)

_____ Job(s)

_____ Sexual intimacy

_____ Pornography

_____ Anger problems

_____ Lack of forgiveness—specifically: _____

_____ Unresolved issues—specifically: _____

_____ Other: _____

_____ Other: _____

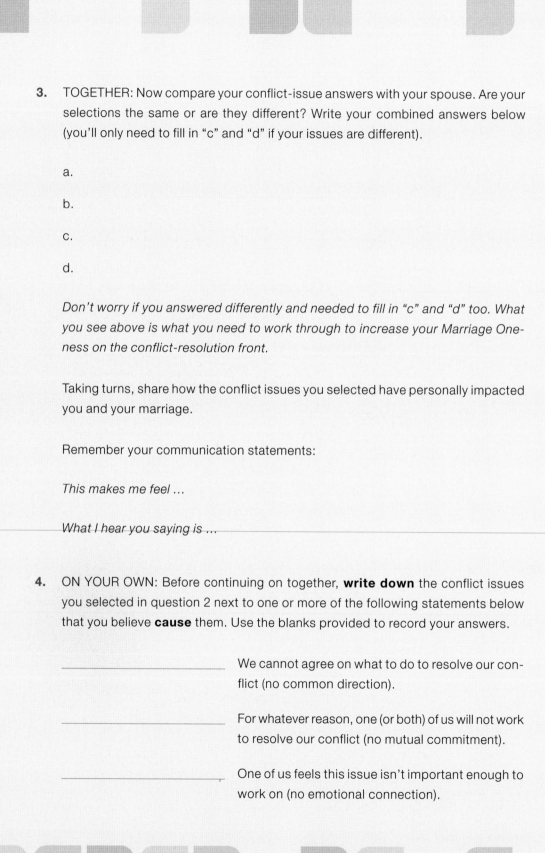

3. TOGETHER: Now compare your conflict-issue answers with your spouse. Are your selections the same or are they different? Write your combined answers below (you'll only need to fill in "c" and "d" if your issues are different).

a.

b.

c.

d.

Don't worry if you answered differently and needed to fill in "c" and "d" too. What you see above is what you need to work through to increase your Marriage One-ness on the conflict-resolution front.

Taking turns, share how the conflict issues you selected have personally impacted you and your marriage.

Remember your communication statements:

This makes me feel …

What I hear you saying is …

4. ON YOUR OWN: Before continuing on together, **write down** the conflict issues you selected in question 2 next to one or more of the following statements below that you believe **cause** them. Use the blanks provided to record your answers.

_____ We cannot agree on what to do to resolve our conflict (no common direction).

_____ For whatever reason, one (or both) of us will not work to resolve our conflict (no mutual commitment).

_____ One of us feels this issue isn't important enough to work on (no emotional connection).

_____ One (or both) of us refuses to change or compromise (no mutual commitment).

_____ We don't know what to do about this conflict (no common direction). We stay defensive and lack the skills necessary to resolve it.

_____ We know what to do, but one (or both) of us fails to follow through (no mutual commitment).

_____ One (or both) of us won't ask for forgiveness (no emotional connection).

_____ One (or both) of us won't forgive (no emotional connection).

_____ Other: _____

5. TOGETHER: Talk about the conflict-cause matches you made above. Listen closely to each other. What new insights did you gain? Use the space below to record the most important ones.

6. TOGETHER: What immediate changes could we make to better address each of these conflicts, at least on a basic level? Write down these changes in the space below.

7. TOGETHER: What possible next step could we take together to further improve our Marriage Oneness in this important area of conflict resolution? (Remember, if you're having trouble answering this one, there are suggestions on pages 35 and 126.) Turn to your **Next Steps Planner** at the back of the book to record your answer.

success**story**

conflict resolution

Michael & Jill DeLon

Everyone knows that when opposites attract, fireworks are bound to occur. But when opposites vow to remain together "until death parts us," conflict resolution becomes key to helping the marriage survive.

"Jill and I are *complete* opposites," Michael says, "and the cultures in our extended families were equally dissimilar. Jill is logical. I'm emotional. Jill has seven reasons why her way is 'right.' I don't have any reasons, just a gut feeling (that holds no water against logic!). She comes from a family where conflict is normal …"

"I wouldn't say conflict was normal," Jill says. "I grew up in a home where everyone spoke their minds."

"But heated discussions were pretty normal, right?"

"Right."

Michael slips his hand into Jill's. "For us, divorce was never an option; but living together in isolation was becoming a very real threat. Our first five years of our marriage were filled with what I felt was constant tension. It was like walking on eggshells for me. If I would say the wrong thing or make a decision that she didn't like, she was quick to confront me and let me know why I was wrong."

"I didn't set out to cause conflict," Jill says. "I thought I was just voicing my opinion."

"And I didn't know how to respond, so I acquiesced. I hoped our conflicts would simply go away in time."

"If Michael had been a person who met conflict head-on, I think we would have had terrible fights. I mean *big* arguments. But Michael remained calm, so I thought everything was okay."

The DeLons continued on in this way, not fighting, but inwardly drawing apart for reasons they couldn't quite name. They could feel the separation, but because things seemed on target from the outside, they thought their marriage was pretty normal. That was until they went to a Weekend to Remember getaway in 1995.

"It was like the light went on," Michael says. "Although I had grown up in the church, no one had ever taught me that God had a plan for marriage. We listened, talked, purchased books, and came away with a renewed vision and a proven plan for how our marriage could and should be."

Jill agrees. "God really opened my eyes to my self-centeredness, anger, and unrealistic expectations, and I began to change."

But Jill wasn't the only one who had to change.

44

Michael found he needed to assume a role of leadership and find ways to address conflict rather than dodge it. "I remember cutting out a page from the manual and sticking it to our refrigerator," he says. "Those steps to resolving conflict became a guide to us on a regular basis."

As their discussions heated up, the DeLons reviewed those steps, learning to address issues without picking sides and how to truly listen.

"But another real change," Jill says, "was when I accepted that there is more than one way to accomplish a task. It seems obvious now, but for me it was huge 'aha.' I really learned to trust my husband and, ultimately, to trust God working in his life. That let *me* let *go.* And I think another big thing for us was learning how to forgive."

Michael agrees. "Forgiveness is a choice. It's a matter of giving up my right to seek revenge when I've been hurt. It's part of extending grace to another."

Fifteen years later, the DeLons still have disagreements and are quick to acknowledge that they don't always handle conflict properly, but they feel confident in knowing how to resolve their issues, forgive, and move on.

"Jill and I are still opposites," Michael says. "Fortunately, like two magnets, we've learned to 'align our poles' to attract—rather than repel—each other."

suggested resources

Looking for more information on the subject of conflict resolution?

Fight Fair!
by Tim and Joy Downs

So often when couples fight, tempers flare … tongues loosen … and behavior occurs that can cause major damage. Get practical tips and expert advice that you can apply to ensure that future conflicts don't create permanent scars. Help make your conflicts—and your marriage—a win-win.

One of Us Must Be Crazy … and I'm Pretty Sure It's You
by Tim and Joy Downs

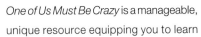

One of Us Must Be Crazy is a manageable, unique resource equipping you to learn the true nature of your conflicts and deal with them in a way that increases marital fulfillment. By interacting candidly with issues like security, loyalty, responsibility, caring, order, openness, and connection, this new way to fight might make all the difference.

Peacemaking for Families
by Ken Sande

We all long for a home that is a haven from a world riddled by conflict. But even in a family, conflict is inevitable. Learn to be peacemakers and help guard your family from destructive conflict. Deepen your love and intimacy with your spouse, and provide your children with a solid foundation for life.

money

and marriage oneness

Let's Get Real About Money

(A)   How we act with our money and why

1.   Personal history shapes how we approach money.

2.   Personal "bent" shapes how we handle money.

---

bring it home

Mark where you think you fall on the Spender–Saver Scale.

Spender									Saver
1	2	3	4	5	6	7	8	9	10

(B)   Where we are with our money and why

1.   A major problem for most couples:
     money _____ .

2.   Information is your ally when it comes to money.

Tim & Joy

Q: How do your backgrounds affect how you handle money?

Joy: I grew up with a father who taught us to save for what was ahead, so when Tim and I came together, it was a little bit of a struggle.

Tim: It took a while for us to learn that when it comes to money, we're really talking about deeper issues. Joy has more of a desire for security than I do; I tend to just want to enjoy the day. Joy wants to enjoy the day too, but she also wants to make sure that we're going to be okay tomorrow. I had to become better at organizing and budgeting to help her feel secure.

II. Major Money Mistakes That Couples Commonly Make

(A) A _____ lifestyle

(B) Excessive _____ _____ debt

(C) Unwise _____ purchases

(D) The non-existent _____

(E) A lack of _____

> "A budget is people telling their money where to go instead of wondering where it went."[1]
>
> —**John Maxwell**

III. The Bible and Money

(A) Money is a frequent topic of Scripture.

(B) Four major money themes in Scripture

1. _____ **money**

2. _____ **money**

3. _____ **money**

4. _____ **money**

IV. The Bible's Live-Give-Save-Limit Wisdom

(A) Live it _____!

1. Enjoy life together ...

"To every man whom God has given wealth and possessions, he has also given him the ability to eat from them, to receive his reward and to find enjoyment in his toil; these things are the gift of God." —ECCLESIASTES 5:19 (NET)

2.   ... but live wisely.

▶   Live according to a _____.

▶   Beware of budget busters, *especially* _____
     _____.

     Wait 48 hours to think about all big purchases!

3.   Recommendation: Seek to live on _____ of your income.

(B)   Always _____ something.

1.   Giving transforms your life and makes you a better person.

"Remember the words of the Lord Jesus, that He Himself said, 'It is more blessed to give than to receive.'" —ACTS 20:35

2.   **Giving is the key to controlling your money instead of being controlled by it.**

"One person is generous and yet grows more wealthy, but another withholds more than he should and comes to poverty. A generous person will be enriched, and the one who provides water for others will himself be satisfied." —PROVERBS 11:24-25 (NET)

3.   **Give _____ before you spend.**

"Honor the LORD from your wealth and from the first of all your produce." —PROVERBS 3:9

4.   Recommendation: Seek to give _____ of your income away.

(C) Always _____ something.

"There is precious treasure and oil in the dwelling of the wise, but a foolish man swallows it up." —PROVERBS 21:20

1. **Immediate: An emergency fund**
    - ▶ Every couple would be wise to have one thousand dollars put away for the unexpected emergency.
    - ▶ When used, replace it immediately.

2. **Intermediate: Back-up savings**
    - ▶ Equal to three months of household expenses
    - ▶ Put in place before going long-term

3. **Long-term: Future savings**
    - ▶ Retirement—financial independence
    - ▶ Kids—college tuition, weddings, etc.
    - ▶ Dreams—trips, goals, experiences

4. **Recommendation: Seek to save _____ of your income.**

(D) Limit _____.

"The rich rules over the poor, and the borrower becomes the lender's slave." —PROVERBS 22:7

1. **Debt will be a constant struggle.**
2. **Self-control now leads to greater freedom later.**
3. **The best way to deal with debt is to _____ it.**
    - ▶ List all of your debts, smallest at the top. Pay the minimum on all bills, and then any extra you can on the top one, and you'll begin to pay them off.

4. **Recommendation: Limit debt to only what you are _____ you can pay back.**

V Experiencing Oneness with Money

(A) You both must be committed to experience good money results.

    1. Create a budget and stick to it.

    2. When you need help or advice, be smart and ask for it.

        ▶ Successful people seek out wise money advisors.

(B) Good money management will energize oneness in your marriage.

> *"Agree on a budget with your spouse ... If you aren't working together, it is almost impossible to win."* [5]
>
> **—Dave Ramsey**

Bryan & Korie

Q: How has money brought you together? Or driven you apart?

Bryan: I've learned I need to give Korie the freedom that she needs to be able to spend within reason. But on the other hand, you know, I am always thinking down the road, and I can be, uh, a little bit *frugal*.

Korie: You mean *cheap*.

Bryan: Early on we got into some foolish debt, and it took a while to get out of it. Coming through that kind of experience can lead to another challenge on the other side of the pendulum—you have to figure out the difference between being responsible and hoarding.

Korie: Now we each get a little spending money each month that we can use as we see fit—without checking in with each other. That's worked well—for both of us.

circle**up** ...

(3 couples max)

Choose a volunteer to lead your group through the following questions. Remember your small-group discussion guidelines:

- ▶ **Everyone participates.**
- ▶ **No one dominates.**
- ▶ **No one embarrasses his or her spouse.**

1. What was one of the most significant things you learned in this session about money? Explain.

2. Where do you and your spouse fall on the Spender-Saver Scale presented in this session? How have the differences (if any) between you and your spouse on this scale affected your marriage?

3. What is one financial mistake you wish you hadn't made?

4. As a couple, do you currently have a money game plan (i.e., budget) you are committed to using in your marriage? If yes, how has it helped you? Explain.

5. What spoke to you the most from the Bible's live-give-save-limit wisdom on money? (Live it up, but wisely; give something; save something; limit debt.)

Onenesswork

This week's OnenessWork is designed to help you, as a couple, do two things. First, it provides a way for you to document how you use your money and where. Second, it gives you the opportunity to analyze your money expenditures and then make whatever changes you think are needed.

Before your date ...

Whoever manages the money in your marriage must first do some investigative financial research into your spending habits. This will take some extra time and effort, **but it is critical to the success of this OnenessWork assignment!**

To prepare, you or your spouse will need to fill out the **Where Our Money Is Going Monthly Summary** found on the pages that follow. An electronic copy can be found online at LifeReady.com/marriageoneness/budget. For this summary to be accurate, you'll need to carefully review your monthly spending habits using your checkbooks, debit and credit-card statements, and online banking records. Once it's complete, you're ready for your date.

NOTE: *If you or your spouse find the assignment of filling out the **Where Our Money Is Going Monthly Summary** confusing or overwhelming, then stop. It would be best to wait until this Marriage Oneness series is over and then seek outside assistance to help you put together a budget you can understand and use. (This doesn't mean you're "failing"; it just means you need help on this front. Lots of us do!) If you think this describes you, skip the monthly summary interaction and use your money date to answer only the following discussion questions.*

On your date ...

1. For your OnenessWork date, you'll need two hours in a quiet, comfortable setting.

2. For many couples, money is a difficult subject. A good way to begin this date is by reading together the following prayer:

   Heavenly Father, we want to be wise in the way we use our money. Help us now to find ways to do that together. Help us move closer to financial oneness. In Jesus' name. Amen.

3. Before looking over your **Where Our Money Is Going Monthly Summary** together, answer the following discussion questions:

   ▶ Is there anything you wish you knew more about when it comes to handling money?

   I wish I knew more about:

   My spouse wishes he or she knew more about:

   ▶ What is your biggest money worry at present, and how does it affect you?

   My biggest worry:

   It affects me this way:

   My spouse's biggest worry:

   Effect on spouse:

▶ If, as a couple, you had to cut back on spending, what three areas would you choose? What three areas would you keep as-is in your current budget? Decide together:

CUT #1:

CUT #2:

CUT #3:

KEEP AS-IS #1:

KEEP AS-IS #2:

KEEP AS-IS #3:

▶ What one thing could you personally do or change right now to better handle money in your marriage?

I could …

My spouse thinks he or she could …

4. Now discuss your spending habits. Whoever researched your spending habits should first explain what he or she found by going over the completed **Where Our Money Is Going Monthly Summary**. Discuss these findings so that each of you has a clear understanding. Then address the following questions:

▶ Are there any surprises in your summary? Where?

▶ Are there any warnings in your summary? Where?

▶ What is pleasing about how you use your money?

▶ What do you need to reconsider, alter, or stop concerning how you use your money?

5. Now look at the **Where We Would Like Our Money to Go Monthly Budget**.

What changes do you want to make right now regarding how you use your money? What specific steps will you need to take to make these changes a reality? Discuss and then record your changes in this new budget. If you need more time to finish this budget discussion, set a time to meet again. Then let this new budget, and further refinement to it, guide you in the months ahead.

6. What possible next step could you take together to further improve your Marriage Oneness in this important area of money? Turn to your **Next Steps Planner** and record your answer. (Note: If you were not able to complete the **Where Our Money Is Going Monthly Summary**, then your next step should be to seek out someone who can help you understand and use a budget.)

where our money is going monthly summary

1. Give:
Church _____
Charities _____
Individuals _____
Total Giving: _____

2. Save:
Retirement _____
College Fund _____
Emergency Fund _____
Other _____
Total Savings: _____

3. Live:

Housing:
Mortgage / Rent _____
Taxes / Insurance _____
Electricity _____
Gas / Heating Oil _____
Water _____
Telephone _____
Cell Phone(s) _____
Cleaning _____
Cable / Satellite TV _____
Internet _____
Repairs / Maintenance _____
Furniture / Decorations / Improvements _____
Termite / Pest Control _____
Other _____
Total Housing: _____

Transportation:
Public Transportation _____
Car Payments _____
Gasoline _____
Parking _____
Repairs / Maintenance _____
Insurance _____
Personal Property Taxes / Licenses _____
Total Transportation: _____

Entertainment and Recreation:
Eating Out _____
Babysitting _____
Activities / Hobbies _____
Trips / Vacations _____
Music / Books / DVDs _____
Other _____
Total Entertainment and Recreation: _____

Medical and Dental:
Doctors and Dentists _____
Prescriptions _____
Co-payments _____
Other _____
Total Medical and Dental: _____

Groceries and Household:
Groceries _____
Household Supplies _____
Other _____
Total Groceries and Household: _____

Clothing and Personal Items:
Clothes Purchases _____
Shoes _____
Cosmetics _____
Laundry and Cleaning _____
Hair Salon/Barber _____
Alimony _____
Child Support _____
Total Clothing and Personal Items: _____

Insurance:
Life _____
Health (if not withheld from paycheck) _____
Disability _____
Other _____
Total Insurance: _____

Gifts:
Friends _____
Family _____
Total Gifts: _____

Education and Children:
Tuition / Books / Etc. _____
College Room and Board _____
Child Care _____
Camps and Activities _____
Lessons _____
Lunches _____
Allowances _____
Other _____
Total Education and Children: _____

Miscellaneous:
Pets _____
Magazines / Newspapers _____
Yard Care _____
Other _____
Total Miscellaneous: _____
Total Living Expenses: _____

4. Limit Debt:
Total Credit Card Payments _____
Total Loan Repayments _____
Other _____
Total Debt Payments: _____

Summary

Combined Monthly Income
(after taxes) + _____

Where Our Money Is Going
(add totals 1-4) − _____

Monthly Margin or Deficit = _____

where we would like our money to go monthly budget

1. Give:

Church _____
Charities _____
Individuals _____
Total Giving: _____

2. Save:

Retirement _____
College Fund _____
Emergency Fund _____
Other _____
Total Savings: _____

3. Live:

Housing:

Mortgage / Rent _____
Taxes / Insurance _____
Electricity _____
Gas / Heating Oil _____
Water _____
Telephone _____
Cell Phone(s) _____
Cleaning _____
Cable / Satellite TV _____
Internet _____
Repairs / Maintenance _____
Furniture / Decorations / Improvements _____
Termite / Pest Control _____
Other _____
Total Housing: _____

Transportation:

Public Transportation _____
Car Payments _____
Gasoline _____
Parking _____
Repairs / Maintenance _____
Insurance _____
Personal Property Taxes / Licenses _____
Total Transportation: _____

Entertainment and Recreation:

Eating Out _____
Babysitting _____
Activities / Hobbies _____
Trips / Vacations _____
Music / Books / DVDs _____
Other _____
Total Entertainment and Recreation: _____

Medical and Dental:

Doctors and Dentists _____
Prescriptions _____
Co-payments _____
Other _____
Total Medical and Dental: _____

Groceries and Household:

Groceries _____
Household Supplies _____
Other _____
Total Groceries and Household: _____

Clothing and Personal Items:

Clothes Purchases _____
Shoes _____
Cosmetics _____
Laundry and Cleaning _____
Hair Salon/Barber _____
Alimony _____
Child Support _____
Total Clothing and Personal Items: _____

Insurance:

Life _____
Health (if not withheld from paycheck) _____
Disability _____
Other _____
Total Insurance: _____

Gifts:

Friends _____
Family _____
Total Gifts: _____

Education and Children:

Tuition / Books / Etc. _____
College Room and Board _____
Child Care _____
Camps and Activities _____
Lessons _____
Lunches _____
Allowances _____
Other _____
Total Education and Children: _____

Miscellaneous:

Pets _____
Magazines / Newspapers _____
Yard Care _____
Other _____
Total Miscellaneous: _____

Total Living Expenses: _____

4. Limit Debt:

Total Credit Card Payments _____
Total Loan Repayments _____
Other _____
Total Debt Payments: _____

Summary

Combined Monthly Income
(after taxes)
$+$ _____

Where We Would Like Our Money to Go
(add totals 1-4)
$-$ _____

Monthly Margin or Deficit
$=$ _____

An electronic file version of these spreadsheets is available in Excel on our Web site. If you'd prefer to fill these out on your computer so that they can be easily updated, go to LifeReady.com/marriageoneness/budget.

successstory

money and marriage oneness

"George is a spender and I am a saver," Isabel says, "so needless to say, this caused some tension in our home." George and Isabel* were a little more than a year into their marriage and living what they believed was the American dream, with two incomes, a new car, and plans to build a new home.

"We had already racked up more than $70,000 in debt, not including our mortgage. Luckily, we had a good friend who encouraged us to try the Financial Peace University class first. We agreed, not thinking it would change anything." But in fact, it changed everything.

George and Isabel finished the class and decided "that we didn't want our money—or lack thereof—to control us." That meant they had to cancel their plans to build the new house, commit to live on a budget, and start to pay off their debts. "We hadn't realized the pressure we had put on ourselves by buying more than we could afford."

The couple found strength in their common goal (becoming debt free) and worked at it together. Isabel says, "We worked second jobs, had garage sales, sold things, and did anything we could do for extra money. We were approaching the end, when a surprise pregnancy kicked us into even higher gear. I knew that I wanted to be able to stay at home with my child."

It took three and a half years, but they were able to pay off all their debt. They say they gained in so many ways, not just learning to live within their means. "We learned to work as a team," George says, "and we eliminated so much stress in our marriage."

The key? "We realized that we had to decide to put our marriage and family above our wants and desires for things," Isabel says. "No home, car, or any possession is worth the load we were carrying. I was able to quit my job and stay at home with my child, all because we learned how to manage our money." It would never have been an option for them if they had continued with their old spending habits. "Now, if we want something, we save up and pay cash. Being financially secure has brought us both tremendous peace."

George and Isabel maintain that financial peace is possible even when one spouse is a "spender" and the other is a "saver." They worked this out by consistently setting aside funds for George's "spending-money account" and Isabel's "savings account."

62

For the saver in the family, it was really about feeling secure. For the spender in the family it was really about feeling some freedom, now and again, to splurge. Together, they decide on what they want as a family and save toward it. "This way we don't go into debt, which stresses me out," Isabel says, "and we actually get to enjoy spending without guilt. We realize our differences can be a benefit to our marriage, and with some careful management, we've become a team on the financial front."

The story told here is true, although names and other details have been changed to conceal identities.

suggestedresources

Looking for more information on the subject of money?

Total Money Makeover
by Dave Ramsey
Instead of the normal dose of quick fixes, Ramsey offers a bold, no-nonsense approach to money matters — with not only the how-to but also a grounded and uplifting hope for getting out of debt and achieving total financial health. Ramsey debunks the many myths of money and attacks the illusions and downright deceptions of the American dream. "Don't even consider keeping up with the Joneses," Ramsey declares candidly. "They're broke!"

Your Money Map
by Howard Dayton
Finding your way to any destination requires a map — including your financial destination. Based on the phenomenally popular Money Map concept created by Crown Ministries, you'll discover a simple road map for organizing finances throughout life.

Financial Peace University

Dave Ramsey's life-changing program teaches you to practically achieve your financial goals by eliminating debt, saving for the future, and giving like never before. More than one million families have attended FPU with amazing results. You'll be challenged, and motivated to make a plan for your money that changes your family tree forever.

Go to daveramsey.com/fpu to learn more about Financial Peace University.

spiritual beliefs

and marriage oneness

I Spiritual Anxieties

(A) You are not sure what your spouse *believes* spiritually.

(B) You and your spouse have *different* religious backgrounds and/or differing spiritual beliefs and interests that create tension in your marriage.

(C) You and your spouse struggle with *how* to make spiritual life work practically in your marriage.

Bryan & Korie

Q: What advice do you have in regard to spirituality and marriage?

Bryan: You've got to own your walk with Christ. I grew up in a home where that was modeled by two great parents; I saw the effects it had for them and on us, and that still impacts me and mine today. So I think one of the greatest gifts I can give my wife is a life that is personally invested in and committed to figuring out what I believe about the Scriptures and Christ.

Korie: And I encourage couples to go to God's Word when you're facing a disagreement, to look up for yourself what God has to say about the matter; find the truth and then pray you can come together on the matter, based on that truth. We've found that many of our "differences" disappear when using this approach.

II Some Perspectives on Spiritual Beliefs in Marriage

(A) The Good

▶ Couples who regularly go to church together have much lower divorce rates and happier marriages.

(B) The Bad

▶ Couples who have different spiritual beliefs have a divorce rate three times higher than other couples.

▶ It's much harder to have soul-level harmony without soul-level belief.

(C) The Very Good

▶ The happiest married couples are those who share a common spiritual life together.

III What Spiritual Oneness Is and Isn't in a Marriage

(A) Spiritual Oneness is more than a _passive_ acknowledgment of God together.

(B) Spiritual Oneness is more than attending church together.

(C) Spiritual Oneness is not spiritual _sameness_.

(D) Spiritual Oneness is a husband and wife mutually committed to believing and following Jesus Christ. This mutual commitment then leads to a shared and exciting spiritual journey.

Tim & Joy

Q: How has faith impacted you and your marriage? How do you advise others?

Joy: Having a community of believers around us, and particularly for me—to have a couple of good girlfriends that I can talk to, who let me know that my marriage is not the only one that has some struggles—that's been a great encouragement for me.

Tim: We're different in so many ways, and we have spiritual differences as well. Attending church or being in a Bible study together gives us a chance to consider a subject or thought, talk about it, and find out what we have in common or where we come at things a different way.

Joy: If you're on different pages spiritually, try to be patient with the other person and pray you would be a reflection of God's love to them. Even that circumstance is something God can use to strengthen your own spiritual life.

IV **What Spiritual Oneness Looks Like**

(A)   A common model of marriage

Husband   Wife

(B)   God's model of marriage

"Two are better than one because they have a good return for their labor. For if either of them falls, the one will lift up his companion. ... If two lie down together they keep warm, but how can one keep warm alone? ... A cord of three strands is not quickly torn apart."
—ECCLESIASTES 4:9-12

"Our circumstances don't determine our contentment, but our faith and trust in God do ... If we are in the center of God's will for our lives, we can bear up under any amount of stress."[3]

—Patrick M. Morley

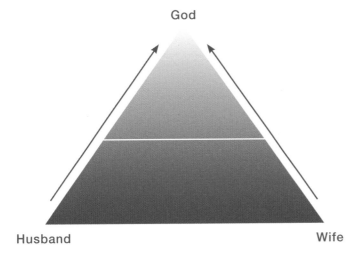

1.   We yield together to God's higher authority (mutual commitment).

2.   We pursue together the wisdom of God's Word (common direction).

3.   We enjoy together spiritual experiences one or both of us have had (emotional connection).

V Four Ways to Strengthen Spiritual Life in Your Marriage

(A) As a couple you should seek to know and understand the Bible.

"How blessed is the man who ... [delights] in the law of the LORD. And in His law he meditates day and night. He will be like a tree firmly planted by streams of water, which yields its fruit in its season and its leaf does not wither; and in whatever he does, he prospers." —PSALM 1:1-3

1. Commit first to reading the Bible for yourself on a regular basis.

2. Share your discoveries in the Bible with your spouse.

3. Join a couples group and study the Bible together.

(B) _Pray_ together.

"Be anxious for nothing, but in everything by prayer and supplication with thanksgiving let your requests be made known to God. And the peace of God, which surpasses all comprehension, will guard your hearts and your minds in Christ Jesus." —PHILIPPIANS 4:6-7

1. Praying together builds a unique emotional intimacy.

2. If you've never done this before, start by sharing a one _sentence_ _prayer_ together at bedtime.

> "In a University of Chicago study [of married couples], 75 percent of the Americans who pray with their spouses reported that their marriages are 'very happy' ... Those who pray together are also more likely to say they respect each other, discuss their marriage together, and— stop the presses— rate their spouses as skilled lovers."[4]
>
> —Ty Wenger

(C) Worship together.

*"... not forsaking our own assembling together, as is the habit
of some, but encouraging one another ..."* —HEBREWS 10:25

1. Find a good church that encourages you both. Regular
worship together will strengthen your marriage.

2. Husbands, show your spiritual leadership here. Make
finding a good church and going to church regularly
your responsibility.

(D) Share your spiritual thoughts and experiences with each other.

*"Therefore encourage one another and build up one
another."* —1 THESSALONIANS 5:11

VI How You Can Have a Spiritual Life

*"Behold, I [Jesus] stand at the door and knock: if any man
hear my voice and open the door, I will come in to him."*
—REVELATION 3:20 (ASV)

*"I have come that they
may have life, and have
it to the full."*

—Jesus (John 10:10, NIV)

**We have to open the door. If you've never asked Jesus to be a
part of your life, here's one way you can do so:**

Dear God,

I want to know You and have a real relationship with You.
I believe that You love me and that Jesus died on the cross to pay for my sins.
Please forgive me for all the things that I have done wrong.
From this moment forward I choose to trust You and follow You.
I believe that today marks a new day in my journey as a follower of Jesus.
I pray this in Jesus' name.
Amen.

circleup ...

(3 couples max)

Do not get in a small group during this Circle Up time. This is a time for you as a couple to talk privately about your spiritual beliefs.

Share with each other your answers to the following questions:

1. What was the most helpful thing you heard in this session? Explain.

2. Circle one of the following terms that you think best describes your relationship with God right now.

    ▶ Nowhere

    ▶ Foggy

    ▶ Distant

    ▶ Conflicted

    ▶ Close

    ▶ Growing

    ▶ New

    Now tell your spouse why you picked this word.

3. What is one thing you would want your spouse to know about you spiritually? Explain.

4. What has been your greatest "God moment" — a time when you knew He was really there?

5. If you could change anything about your spiritual life, what would it be? Explain.

Oonenesswork

For your OnenessWork this week, you'll need two hours in a quiet, undisturbed setting. It would be *very helpful* if you would look over the following questions in advance of your date.

On your date ...

Commit to make this a time focused on understanding each other better. Some couples will find it hard to discuss their spiritual beliefs, but don't let fear hold you back. Be courageous and move forward. Also, be sensitive to each other. Where there are spiritual differences, seek greater understanding rather than debating or arguing over them.

1. Begin your date by reading together the following prayer:

    Heavenly Father, help us in our spiritual journey together. Help us to spiritually understand each other and find new ways to grow closer together. In Jesus' name. Amen.

2. Now open your *Marriage Oneness Profile* and look at the section titled Spiritual Beliefs. What do your results say about your spiritual oneness in this area right now?

3. Which **one** of the "discussion items" listed in the Spiritual Beliefs section of your *Marriage Oneness Profile* do you think is most important to talk about? How about your spouse? Identify and then discuss.

My most important discussion item is:

My spouse's most important discussion item is:

4. Briefly tell your spouse your thoughts about each of the following questions:

    ▶ Do you trust what the Bible says? Why or why not?

    ▶ What do you think God is like?

    ▶ Who is Jesus Christ?

    ▶ What is sin?

    ▶ How do we get to heaven?

5. What are some of your greatest unanswered spiritual questions?

6. Is God working in your life right now? In what way or ways have you experienced His presence lately?

7. What are your top spiritual priorities? How do they compare with those of your spouse?

My top three spiritual priorities:

▶

▶

▶

My spouse's top three spiritual priorities:

▶

▶

▶

8. Do your spiritual priorities draw you together as a couple or pull you apart?

9. Do you pray together? If not, would you be willing to take the challenge of starting right now with Tim's suggestion of sharing a one-sentence prayer every night?

10. What possible next step could you take together to further improve your Marriage Oneness in this important area of spiritual beliefs? Turn to your **Next Steps Planner** and record your answer.

spiritual intimacy

Bret & Elizabeth Hern

It took two very dark years and nearly losing their marriage for God to finally get Bret and Elizabeth's attention.

The Herns both grew up in solid, stable, church-going families, but God was never at the center of their lives. Other than going through the requisite motions of getting married and baptizing their two children, faith faded into the background as the demands of career and children took center stage.

When Bret took a job with a start-up company in Austin, Texas, 150 miles away from their home in Houston, he threw himself into the new venture, routinely working hundred-hour weeks. But when the company wanted the Herns to move to Austin, Elizabeth knew the job had become a destructive trap. "I told Bret I wanted to stay in Houston," she says, "that being a 'work widow' wasn't what I had signed up for. But Bret discounted every objection I raised and ultimately made our moving an ultimatum."

Bret says, "I'm embarrassed by it now, partly because of the disastrous results, but mostly because of the pathetic emptiness of my position: 'If you love me and trust me, you'll let me keep *my* dream.'"

As Elizabeth feared, moving to Austin did not restore a balance to their lives, and removed from family, friends, and her own comfort zone,

she took out her frustrations on Bret. "I wanted so much more from our marriage." Their situation worsened until finally, in the midst of yet another argument, Elizabeth threatened a divorce.

"That really scared me," says Bret. "I was willing to try anything to fix it." They sought marriage counseling, and it helped avert the breakup of their marriage.

"The counselor helped us see hope in our situation, that despite our problems, we had a lot going for us," says Elizabeth. But while the marriage had survived the crisis, a lot of hurt remained.

"Bret was talking to another start-up about working with them. It felt like the same thing all over again. It wasn't until he turned them down that I actually believed I could trust him again," says Elizabeth. Instead, Bret took a job that moved the family back to Houston, and enrolled the children in a Christian school.

Eventually, they started to attend church together "for the *kids*," Bret says with a laugh. "But I needed it most of all, of course. Having gone through the turmoil of the previous couple of years, I think I was finally open to the possibility that I didn't have all the answers. It finally sunk in—I wasn't enough, on my own. I needed a relationship with Jesus Christ." He began to study and read the Bible, but he discussed little of his burgeoning faith with Elizabeth.

About a year later, Elizabeth had her own moment of understanding: "I was half asleep one morning and heard a voice saying, 'There really is a God.' That was it. I knew it, deep down, as truth. And it was exactly what I needed to hear."

Elizabeth and Bret began making up for lost time, radically changing their lives, investing more time in spiritual pursuits together and eventually a ministry of their own. At home, they became much more intentional about sharing their faith with their children. "We have wonderful parents, but their faith was always a personal matter. We realized we needed to do things differently," says Elizabeth.

Coming to faith has changed the entire trajectory of Bret and Elizabeth's lives and marriage. "While we struggled through issues like most couples, the real problem for us was that we had no shared vision for our lives," says Bret. "We were committed to staying together—probably driven more by a fear of failure than anything else—but weren't committed to anything bigger than ourselves. Coming to faith in Jesus Christ allowed us to see, accept, and experience His vision for our lives."

suggestedresources

Looking for more information on the subject of spiritual beliefs?

Sacred Marriage
by Gary Thomas

What if God's main intention for your marriage isn't to make you happy, but to make you more like Him? What if He's more interested in changing you than in changing your spouse? Look at your marriage in a different light—as a spiritual discipline and laboratory to cultivate the image of Christ in each other.

Love and Respect
by Emerson Eggerichs

A wife has a driving need: to feel loved. A husband has a driving need: to feel respected. When either of these needs isn't met, things get crazy. *Love and Respect* reveals reasons spouses react negatively to each other—and how they can deal with that conflict quickly, easily, and biblically.

HomeBuilders Couples Series®
Small-Group Study
Building Your Marriage to Last
by Dennis Rainey

Your marriage is under construction every day. No matter how your marriage has been, you, your spouse, and a group of friends can start renovating right now with this seven-week study on *Building Your Marriage to Last,* discovering God's blueprint for your marriage.

sexual intimacy
and marriage oneness

I Big Picture Feedback

(A) Pleasure

(B) Frequency

(C) Duration

(D) Variety

(E) Satisfaction

Bryan & Korie

Q: Quick, what's the best piece of advice you've received in regard to sexual intimacy?

Bryan: I heard a speaker say that for a woman, sex begins at breakfast. I was thinking, *Great, 'cause I'm a morning person.* It didn't take long to realize that wasn't what he meant. Korie just needs to feel treasured and adored all day long—no strings attached, with or without sex at the end—so if my goal is intimacy, I need to send a text message, a quick e-mail, a phone call that tells her I'm really thinking about her, first.

Korie: We have to work at it. It's so easy to get busy. . . . There are times when you may even have to schedule it into your calendar. That's how important it is. And it's important to take care of yourself—men are so visual. Make yourself feel beautiful, and you'll be all the more attractive to your husband.

II Sex Is an Essential Part of Marital Oneness

"Enjoy life with the woman whom you love all the days of your fleeting life which He [God} has given to you under the sun; for this is your reward in life." —ECCLESIASTES 9:9

(A) Sex is a gift God has given a married couple to experience physical pleasure and deep _____ connection with one another.

"Rejoice in the wife of your youth. As a loving hind and a graceful doe, let her breasts satisfy you at all times; be exhilarated always with her love." —PROVERBS 5:18-19

"How beautiful are your sandaled feet, O nobleman's daughter! The curves of your thighs are like jewels, the work of the hands of a master craftsman. Your navel is a round mixing bowl— may it never lack mixed wine! Your belly is a mound of wheat, encircled by lilies. Your two breasts are like two fawns, twins of a gazelle." —SONG OF SOLOMON 7:1-3 (NET)

"The locks of your hair are like royal tapestries—the king is held captive in its tresses. How beautiful you are! How lovely, O love, with your delights! Your stature is like a palm tree and your breasts are like clusters of grapes. I want to climb the palm tree, and take hold of its fruit stalks. May your breasts be like the clusters of grapes, and may the fragrance of your breath be like apricots! May your mouth be like the best wine flowing smoothly for my beloved, gliding gently over our lips as we sleep together." —SONG OF SOLOMON 7:5-9 (NET)

(B) The Bible instructs a husband and wife to mutually _____ each other.

"The marriage bed must be a place of mutuality—the husband seeking to satisfy his wife, the wife seeking to satisfy her husband. Marriage is not a place to 'stand up for your rights.' Marriage is a decision to serve the other, whether in bed or out." —1 CORINTHIANS 7:3-4 (MSG)

"The best sexual relationship is the one that proceeds out of a couple's deep and intimate 'soul bonding.' Show me a couple for whom feelings and thoughts are shared from the innermost levels, and I'll show you a couple ready to have a triumphant sexual relationship." [2]

—**Neil Clark Warren**

III Sexual Oneness Is a Life-long Learning Experience

(A) A good sexual relationship requires that we become a
_____ of our mate.

"Husbands ..., live with your wives in an understanding way."
—1 PETER 3:7

(B) There are few places where we, as husbands and wives, are more different than in our approaches to sex.

IV Understanding Our Differences

(A) We have different sex _____.

1. Most men have a _____ sex drive.

2. Most women have a _____ sex drive.

3. Embrace the differences!

"Sex is not about me. As only God could design it—it works best when we seek to please the other person."

—Tim Lundy

(B) We are _____ differently.

1.   Men are stimulated _____ and _____ .

2.   Women are stimulated _____ and _____ .

3.   Be understanding!

(C) We _____ differently.

1.   A man's narrow focus makes him difficult to distract.

2.   A woman's wider focus causes her to be easily
distracted.

3.   Men can jump to sex as a new thing; women see sex as
the continuation of all that has led up to this moment.

(D) We have different _____ .

1.   Men need _____ in order to feel loving and affectionate
toward their wives.

2.   Women need _____ and _____
to feel excited about having sex with their husbands.

(E) We have different _____ .

1.   Men long to be desired and affirmed
_____ _____ .

2.   Women long to be desired and affirmed
_____ _____ .

*"Guys, she knows you
want sex. What she
wants to know is:
Do you want her?"*

—Tim Lundy

V. Wise Moves Every Couple Can Make

(A) _____ with one another.

    1.   Ask your mate to _____ you how best to make love to him or her.

    2.   Share with your mate your sexual likes and dislikes.

    3.   Sexual communication will increase the likelihood of greater sexual satisfaction in your marriage.

(B) Be _____ in bed.

    1.   Never force anything on your mate that he or she doesn't want to do.

    2.   Stay pain-free.

(C) _____ one another.

    1.   Compliment in the moment.

    2.   Praise "right moves."

(D) Keep _____ sexually.

    1.   Read good books to expand your sexual knowledge and understanding.

    2.   Be open to new ideas and practices.

(E) Ask God to help you be the kind of lover who _____ your mate.

> "Let's be honest: Being able to turn a woman genuinely inside out with pleasure—real pleasure, no faking here—is an esteem booster for any man. Don't deny your husband the satisfaction of becoming the best possible lover to his wife."[4]
>
> **—Karen Linamen**

VI Sexual Stumbling Blocks

(A) Ignorance: Seek good resources! There's no excuse for remaining ignorant.

(B) Selfishness: Don't apply these lessons to your spouse; apply them to yourself. Be the best lover you can be!

(C) The past: Guilt and shame over previous sexual relationships can make the bedroom the "most crowded room in the house."

(D) Pornography: It's poison for a marriage. Don't invite the world into your "safe" place, meant for just the two of you.

(E) Pace of life: Prioritize and guard your sex life.

VII Sexual Oneness Energizes a Marriage

(A) Be committed to grow together sexually.

(B) Even small gains will pay rich dividends in your marriage.

Have you suffered abuse in your past? Many times, healing from sexual abuse requires the help of a trained professional. Check with your pastor or another trusted friend for a recommendation of a godly counselor who specializes in this area.

circleup ...

(3 to a group: husbands with husbands;

wives with wives)

Choose a volunteer to lead your small-group discussion. Answer together the following questions. Please follow your small group discussion guidelines:

► **Everyone participates.**
► **No one dominates.**
► **No one embarrasses his or her spouse.**

1. How did this session make you feel: Encouraged? Embarrassed? Hopeful? Convicted? Enlightened? Affirmed? Excited? Choose one or other descriptions and share why.

2. What sexual misconceptions did you bring into your marriage? Where did those misconceptions come from, and how did they impact your marriage?

3. What one thing have you learned in your marriage that has helped you the most when it comes to experiencing sexual intimacy with your wife or husband?

4. What insights did you receive from this session that could help you be more sexually pleasing to your spouse? Explain.

5. What is your greatest takeaway from this session?

Oonenesswork

For your OnenessWork this week, you'll need one to two hours in a private, safe setting. Look over the following instructions in advance of your time together so that you can be prepared. In this hour, you're going to have the opportunity **to teach** your spouse how to best make love to you. You're also going **to learn** from your spouse how to best make love to him or her. This moment has huge benefits for you both.

To teach ...

- ▶ You must have courage and kindness.

- ▶ You must be specific in your comments.

- ▶ You may want to illustrate or demonstrate.

To learn ...

- ▶ You must be open to hear.

- ▶ You must want to learn.

- ▶ You must be willing to try.

Hesitating? If either of you **cannot** meet the teacher and learner descriptions above, then say so and do not complete this assignment. Instead, use this time to share with each other what you learned from the sexual intimacy session and in your Circle Up discussion. After your interaction, answer the "next step" question and record your answer on page 127.

Good to go? If you both feel you **can** meet the above teacher and learner descriptions, then proceed to the following assignment.

On your date ...

1. Begin your date by reading together the following prayer:

    Heavenly Father, give us the courage we need to be open, honest, and responsive to each other. Help us better understand and appreciate one another so that we might enjoy the sexual intimacy You desire for us in our marriage. In Jesus' name. Amen.

2. Complete the following assignment:

    As the **teacher**, each of you will share your answers to the following statements. As the **learner**, listen carefully to what your spouse tells you. Ask follow-up questions if you need further clarification. Remember, the goal is new and deeper understanding of how you both can better love each other.

    ▶   **Warm-up**

        Finish the sentence:

        I feel most attracted to you when ...

        My spouse is most attracted to me when ...

    ▶   **Setting**

        Finish the sentence:

        I like it when ...

            the room is like this ...

the lights are like this …

the temperature of the room is …

you are dressed like …

My spouse likes it when …

the room is like this…

the lights are like this …

the temperature of the room is …

I am dressed like …

▶ **Timing**

Circle one response in each statement:

I like to make love best during [the morning/afternoon/evening/night].

I like to have [an hour's/several hours'/a day's/no advance notice] that my spouse is thinking of making love.

My spouse likes to make love best during this time of day:

My spouse likes to have _____ advance notice that I'm interested in making love.

6

▶ **Enjoyment**

Finish these sentences:

I like it when you approach me this way …

I like it when you talk to me this way …

I like it when we begin this way …

I like it when you touch me this way …

I like it when you remember little things like this …

My spouse likes this approach:

My spouse likes when I talk like this:

My spouse likes to begin this way:

My spouse likes it when I touch him/her this way:

My spouse likes it when I remember these things:

3. What possible next step could you take together to further improve your Marriage Oneness in this important area of sexual intimacy? Turn to your **Next Steps Planner** and record your answer.

success**story**

sexual intimacy

John & Janel Breitenstein

"**When I lie down,** what I really want to do is *sleep*," Janel Breitenstein laughs. She and John have four children ... and the oldest is five. Out of necessity, romance and sex have become more strategic. "I remember reading the question once, 'How do I make love when children are wrapped around my knees?' Now I understand why that's an issue. It's hard enough to find time to *shower* on my own."

The Breitensteins have experimented with initiating romance at different times of the day than the "dead-tired" late night. They've also become deliberate in making the most of opportunities and balancing priorities. Janel says, "Spontaneity has been an energy injection for us—when the mood hits, go for it if at all possible! A little morning romance in an otherwise sleeping house is never a bad way to start the day." She grins. "And our kids don't watch much TV on weekdays, so they're easily glued to a DVD on a weekend. DVD + baby nap time = us time."

But both acknowledge that creating true intimacy goes far beyond the practicalities of time and place. "John has done a lot to create security between us," Janel says. "He really values our being honest with each other—and as we've been married longer, he's learned gentleness to go with it—so I feel safe to tell him what I really think and need. He doesn't feel pressure to give me

compliments I can't believe, so I know that what he says about me and my body is genuine. I feel accepted and beautiful to him, stretch marks and all!"

John notes, "Learning to communicate with that degree of honesty and trust has helped us be more transparent about our wants and needs—as well as more willing to sacrifice for each other. So it's no surprise we've felt even more intimacy and satisfaction."

He adds, "We've both improved at showing each other understanding and just working together to meet both of our needs." Fluency in each others' "love languages" has helped: quality time and physical touch for John; acts of service and words of affirmation for Janel.

Janel agrees. "Sometimes I get selfish. I'm thinking, *Great. Someone else who needs something from me.* But I know that a massage, for example, is a great gift to him. It really makes him feel loved." She also explains, "I'd been advised to 'think sex' throughout the day—since my mind is one of the key factors that makes or breaks things—and even pray for our sex life. Those turned out to be great pieces of advice, especially when I was nursing around the clock and my hormones were bottoming out."

Realizing that exhaustion was sapping her libido, Janel is still working to make the energy for sex a priority, even saying no to other things. "Sex, and my husband, are more important than an empty dishwasher," she chuckles. And since Janel's love languages are acts of service and words of affirmation, John tries to do more of that emptying.

"Life is crazy for us right now," John says. "I get preoccupied, and I can start to take Janel for granted. A breakthrough for me was to really focus on how great my wife was, and how blessed I am. Taking even a minute before I walk in the door to appreciate her in my mind and heart makes it more natural for her to feel cherished. It changes my words so that I'm building her up, and I want to serve her more."

And sometimes, escaping the daily grind can be nothing short of priceless for an energy-starved marriage. John reminisces with a smile: "One of the best things we did recently was to get away for several days without the kids to celebrate our anniversary. The kids not only survived; they benefitted! It was worth every cent. People kept thinking we were honeymooners."

suggestedresources

Looking for more information on the subject of sexual intimacy?

Sheet Music
by Kevin Leman

In *Sheet Music,* psychologist and family expert Dr. Kevin Leman makes it clear: If you and your spouse work in tandem, you'll create some of the most stunning sounds ever heard! All it takes is practice ... and the right attitude, says Dr. Leman. Sex is about the quality of your entire love life, not just the alignment of your bodies.

Simply Romantic Nights 1 & 2

Simply Romantic Nights is designed to add some creative wow! back into your marriage. These romance resource packs are filled with innovative ideas to kindle sensational encounters and encourage intimacy. Both include 24 unique romantic adventures — 12 cards

for him and 12 for her — with complete plans for creative dates, plus a companion book and more.

Intimacy Ignited
by Dr. Joseph and Linda Dillow and Dr. Peter and Lorraine Pintus

After five, ten, or twenty-plus years of marriage, are you and your spouse still experiencing a spark and chemistry in your relationship? Journey through a couple's exploration of the Bible's very own manual on intimacy: The Song of Solomon. Uncover the freedom, holiness, and beauty of the marriage bed.

roles, responsibilities,
and marriage oneness

I. How Do You Decide "Who Does What" in a Marriage?

(A) Every marriage is a small organization.

1. **To be organized means:**

   ▶ Each person has a clear role.

   ▶ Each person has clear responsibilities.

   All great organizations have this kind of clarity.

2. **In marriage, confusion around roles and responsibilities, or the unfair distribution of responsibilities to one mate over another, can quickly undermine a couple's sense of oneness.**

(B) Three questions every married couple must answer for growing in Marriage Oneness:

1. **Can we, as a couple, articulate to one another our specific roles and responsibilities? (Common direction)**

2. **Can we agree that the roles and responsibilities we each have are fair to us? (Emotional connection)**

3. **Are we both committed to fulfilling these roles and responsibilities? (Mutual commitment)**

> *"It's clear today's families are having to negotiate new and dynamic social changes. As more and more women work outside the home, adjustments within the home are both necessary and needed."*
>
> —Tim Lundy

☐☐ The Bible and Marriage Roles

(A) The Bible speaks to _____ roles for husbands and wives to assume in marriage.

(B) The husband's role is one of _____.

1.   In marriage, the Bible calls him the "head."

"For the husband is the head of the wife as Christ is the head of the church." —EPHESIANS 5:23 (NIV)

2.   His role charges him to ...

▶   love and sacrifice for his wife.

"Husbands, love your wives, just as Christ also loved the church and gave Himself up for her." —EPHESIANS 5:25

▶   lead and protect his wife spiritually with God's Word.

[Jesus sanctified His bride, the church,] "having cleansed her by the washing of water with the word, that He might present to Himself the church in all her glory, having no spot or wrinkle or any such thing; but that she would be holy and blameless. So husbands ought also to love their own wives." —EPHESIANS 5:26-28

The husband's role is to make God's Word the standard in the household. He is the "standard bearer."

▶   provide financially for his wife's freedom and security.

"But if anyone does not provide for his own, and especially for those of his household, he has denied the faith." —1 TIMOTHY 5:8

bring it home

Ask your wife, "Do you really want to work?"... and be ready to deal with the answer.

(C) The wife's role is one of _____.

1. In marriage, the Bible calls her a "helper."

"Then the LORD God said, 'It is not good for the man to be alone; I will make him a helper suitable for him.'" —GENESIS 2:18

2. Her role charges her to …

▶ love and support her husband.

"Encourage the young women to love their husbands." —TITUS 2:4

▶ energize her husband with respect.

"And the wife must see to it that she respects her husband." —EPHESIANS 5:33

In action and in speech, embody respect—it will affirm him to be the kind of man you want him to be.

▶ make a good home that encourages him.

"She looks well to the ways of her household … her husband praises her." —PROVERBS 31:27-28

> *"If you want to love your man in the way he needs to be loved, then you need to ensure that he feels your respect most of all."* [1]
>
> **—Shaunti Feldhahn**

(D) These roles work best in a marriage where both husband and wife are _____ to Jesus Christ.

1. Without Jesus Christ, a husband will often lead selfishly and irresponsibly.

2. Without Jesus Christ, a wife will often undermine her husband's leadership and discourage him.

3. Jesus is the key to proper role play.

"Abide in Me, and I in you. As the branch cannot bear fruit of itself unless it abides in the vine, so neither can you unless you abide in Me … He who abides in Me and I in him, he bears much fruit, for apart from Me you can do nothing." —JOHN 15:4-5

III The Bible and Marriage Responsibilities

(A) Beyond roles, the Bible is mostly _____ when it comes to dividing up marriage responsibilities.

The Bible gives you great freedom in dividing up your marriage responsibilities.

(B) So how do you decide who does what in marriage? Below are six practical suggestions:

1. As a couple, make a _____ of all the work required to manage your home well. (You'll have time to do this in your OnenessWork.)

2. Discuss who does what tasks the best and who enjoys certain tasks. Then _____ these with one another.

3. Whatever division of tasks you finally end up with, each of you should feel the division of responsibilities is _____ and balanced.

    There is no 50-50. You both need to give 100 percent!

4. Set agreed-upon _____ for each responsibility.

    ▶ Be realistic, not perfectionistic, about these standards.

    ▶ Consider the season of life you are in. Sometimes standards have to flex for a time.

5. Always be willing to step in and _____ your mate with his or her responsibility when necessary.

    "Through love, serve one another." —GALATIANS 5:13

6. Never forget to express _____ for each other's work.

    ▶ Positive feedback is contagious.

    ▶ Appreciation is an emotional connection that fuels Marriage Oneness.

"Research shows that when men do more of the housework, women's perceptions of fairness and marital satisfaction rise and the couple experiences less marital conflict. Equitable sharing of housework is associated with higher levels of marital satisfaction— and sometimes more sex too! Wives report greater feelings of sexual interest and affection for husbands who participate in housework." [2]

—**Oriel Sullivan and Scott Coltrane**

bring it home
Have you said "thank you" to your spouse today?

Jose & Michelle

Q: How have you two figured out roles and responsibilities?

Michelle: I had to first figure out why God planned it the way he did. God wired men to be the leaders and protectors, and women to be supporters and encouragers.

Q: Was that a struggle?

Michelle: At first, but I've learned that being a help to Jose does not mean that I become a nonperson, that I have no intellectual contribution to make to the family unit. We still sit down and lovingly talk about decisions that we're going to make. I'm included. I'm involved. I'm part of it in the way that I share my thoughts, support, and encouragement.

Jose: So many people really don't understand what it means to be a helper; it is an honoring term. It's as if our family is a baseball team, and I'm manager and Michelle is the coach. I dialogue with her about decisions that need to be made. Sometimes she asks me to trust her; sometimes I ask her to trust me.

Michelle: I think that defining the roles and responsibilities in our marriage has made day-to-day life so much easier. It allows us to operate in peace.

IV The Clearer, the Better

(A) Role and housework confusion are often a major source of conflict in marriage.

(B) If you commit now as a couple to clarify and define your marriage roles and responsibilities, you'll quickly see the positive impact.

1. **Be specific with one another.**

2. **Be fair to one another.**

(C) Clear roles and responsibilities will energize oneness in your marriage.

> *"Successful couples learn to strike a balance, but domestic parity doesn't always mean splitting chores 50-50 ... Those who respect their spouses and appreciate their contributions ... are more likely to be happy and have happy spouses."*[3]
>
> **—Katherine Benenati**

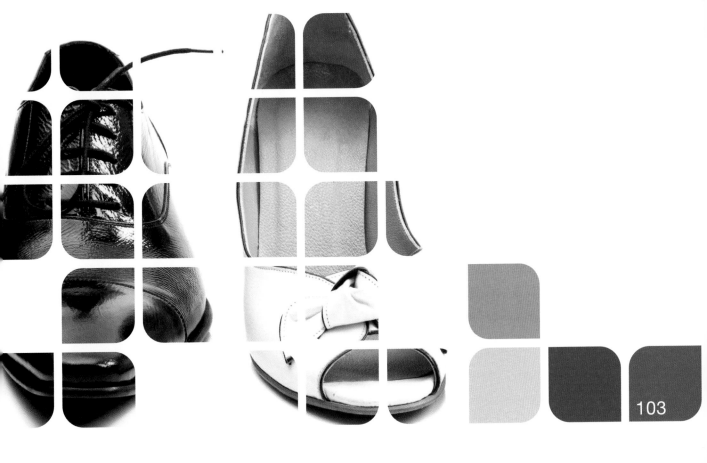

circle**up ...**

(3 couples max)

Choose a volunteer to lead your small-group discussion. Then answer the following questions. Remember your small-group discussion guidelines:

- ▶ **Everyone participates.**
- ▶ **No one dominates.**
- ▶ **No one embarrasses his or her spouse.**

1. Wives, what do you like best about the role the Bible sets forth for husbands? Why?

2. Husbands, what do you like best about the role the Bible sets forth for wives? Why?

3. What do you appreciate the most about the work your spouse does for your household? How does it make you feel?

4. How did you, as a couple, go about deciding "who does what" for your household? Did you discuss it and agree, or did it just happen?

5. Which one of the six practical suggestions Tim gave for dividing up marriage responsibilities most resonated with you (see page 101)? Why?

Oonenesswork

For your OnenessWork this week, you'll need a one to two hour date in a quiet, undisturbed setting.

On your date ...

Focus your time on the responsibilities around your house and how best to divide those responsibilities between you. Remember, the clearer you are on who does what and how, the better you'll do in this area of Marriage Oneness.

1. Begin your date by reading together the following prayer:

    Heavenly Father, help us to find greater oneness and unity in our marriage roles and responsibilities. Give us Your wisdom as we interact together. In Jesus' name. Amen.

2. Open your *Marriage Oneness Profile* and look at the section titled Roles and Responsibilities. What do the results say about your Marriage Oneness in this area?

3. Which **one** of the discussion items listed in your *Profile*'s Roles and Responsibilities section is most important for you to talk about? What about for your spouse? Answer and then discuss.

4. How does your family's unique work situation affect the way you look at dividing up responsibilities?

5. ON YOUR OWN: Before continuing on together, take a moment and individually complete the checklist on page 108.

    Presently in your marriage, who is responsible for the following items? Put your initials by those tasks you believe are your responsibility, your spouse's initials by those you believe are his or her responsibility, both of your initials by those you share, and an X by those you're unsure about.

_____ Paying the bills

_____ Doing laundry

_____ Disciplining
the kids

_____ Cooking

_____ Making the bed

_____ Scheduling
day-to-day
activities

_____ Taking out
the trash

_____ Picking up things
around house

_____ Birthdays and
other celebrations

_____ Car care

_____ Yard work

_____ Shopping

_____ Cleaning up
after meals

_____ Cleaning the
house

_____ Cleaning
bathrooms

_____ Planning
vacations

_____ Taking kids
to school

_____ Repairing the
house

_____ Budgeting
our money

_____ Praying together

_____ Making important
decisions

_____ Helping with
schoolwork

_____ Buying groceries

_____ Bathing the kids

_____ Planning romantic
getaways

_____ Putting the kids
to bed

_____ Scheduling
appointments

_____ Purchasing gifts

_____ Savings and
retirement

_____ Initiating date
nights in order
to spend time
together
communicating

_____ Planning family fun

_____ Attending church

_____ Insurance, will, etc.

Others you feel strongly about ...

_____ Other: _____   _____ Other: _____

_____ Other: _____   _____ Other: _____

_____ Other: _____   _____ Other: _____

6. TOGETHER: Once you have both completed your checklists, compare them together. Discuss any items that don't match or any items you marked with an X.

7. Now go through this checklist again and see if you can clear up any differences or uncertainties. For those items you marked differently than your spouse or for those you marked with an X, discuss these items and decide who will now be responsible for those tasks. Seek to be fair and balanced in how these responsibilities are divided. Where you can't agree, circle that item and leave it. You can address it later on another date.

8. To conclude your OnenessWork, look over your checklist one last time. Is there any item on this list you feel you and your spouse should discuss further to have better agreement on how this responsibility should be carried out? If so, seek now to find a common standard you can both accept and live with.

9. What possible next step could you take together to further improve your Marriage Oneness in this important area of roles and responsibilities? Turn to your **Next Steps Planner** and record your answer.

success**s**tory

roles and responsibilities

Aubrey & Leslie Barner

Growing up as the oldest of four girls, Leslie Barner was taught to get a good education, make her own money, and "never have to depend on a man—something my dad instilled in us. He wanted his daughters to be strong, successful, independent women." Consequently, when she married Aubrey, the last thing Leslie wanted was for him to be the leader in their relationship. "Somehow I had equated that with inferiority for me. And I refuse to be inferior!" she laughs.

"And so, our first few months of marriage," Aubrey says, "was like playing a game of 'Tug-of-War' over the leadership of our home."

Needless to say, for the Barners, almost every major discussion or decision turned into a conflict. Until one particular conflict changed everything. "After about six months of marriage, I made a decision that I stood firm on," says Aubrey. "It was something I felt strongly about, and I was not going to back down."

"That meant that for the first time in our relationship," Leslie says, "I wasn't going to get my way."

"Which didn't go over very well," says Aubrey, laughing.

"I threw a royal fit!" Leslie admits. "You know, the kind a child throws, commonly known as a temper tantrum? Looking back, I can't believe I acted that way."

But through the entire event, Aubrey stood his ground and kept his composure. "After it was over, I said nothing about what had just happened. Instead, I gave her a kiss, looked into her eyes, and said, 'I love you,' then left for work."

Touched by Aubrey's unconditional love at a time when she was being so unlovable, Leslie fell to the floor and cried. "I couldn't believe what he had just done," she says. "There were so many ways Aubrey could've responded, but he had chosen to respond with love. Not only did his response make me feel *truly* loved; he gained my utmost respect—a respect that has not wavered since."

Shortly thereafter, Aubrey and Leslie made a decision for Christ and discovered the biblical blueprints for marriage and family. Aubrey says, "We learned that as husband and wife, we are called to specific God-given roles in marriage."

Leslie adds, "And I learned that even though our roles and responsibilities are different, we are equally valued by God. That understanding combined with our love and respect for each other made embracing those roles easy. 'Yielding' to my husband's leadership was no longer unthinkable, but an honor I embraced. My whole outlook had changed."

As the Barners moved into their God-given roles of servant-leader and lover-helper, they began to experience a harmony they never dreamed possible. "It was as if two out-of-tune instruments finally began to play in sync, and the music they made was beautiful," Leslie says.

"We each took on the household responsibilities that best fit our individual gifts and abilities," Aubrey says, "which has worked really well for us."

Leslie agrees. "Aubrey manages our finances, which is best for our family. If I'd been managing the money, like I had originally insisted, we'd most likely be in a world of trouble," she laughs. "When appropriate, we sometimes trade off responsibilities, others we share ... whatever is needed to best serve each other."

The Barners treasure the harmony and intimacy they have experienced in their marriage. Even when conflict arises, or they are facing difficult times, they work together to guard their relationship and make sure that they *both* win. "I love that my wife has given me the respect and support I need to lead our family well," says Aubrey. "It means more to me than words could ever express."

"And I consider the strong and tender way that Aubrey loves and cherishes me as one of my greatest blessings in life," Leslie says. Their daughters jokingly complain that the two still act like dreamy newlyweds, even after twenty-nine years of marriage. "What can I say?" Leslie asks with a smile. "I am my king's queen."

suggestedresources

Looking for more information on the subject of roles and responsibilities?

For Men Only
by Jeff and Shaunti Feldhahn
So you've been trying to figure her out. Well, now you've got the key to unlock the secrets behind her mysterious ways. Discover for yourself revelations that will help you love your wife and understand her needs.

For Women Only
by Shaunti Feldhahn
Do you have a hard time understanding why men behave the way they do? Do you ever wish you could get inside the mind of your husband? Discover eye-opening revelations that will help you understand how to love and appreciate your man for who he is.

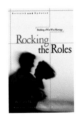

Rocking the Roles
by Robert Lewis
The idea of a marriage without roles sounds noble ... but ultimately fails to deliver on its bright promise. Marriages can be changed when couples understand and embrace their God-given roles in marriage—roles that can help build a win-win marriage.

HomeBuilders Couples Series® Small-Group Study Building Teamwork in Your Marriage
by Robert Lewis and Dave Boehi
Opposites really do attract! And it's the differences that make couples a better team. Learn your biblical roles in this 6-week small-group study and see your spouse as your teammate, not an opponent—growing closer and stronger in your marriage.

family, friends,

and marriage oneness

I Relationships Around Any Marriage Are of Great Importance

(A) They can make vital contributions that bless and enhance a marriage.

> *"A friend loves at all times, and a brother is born for adversity."* —PROVERBS 17:17

(B) They can also create problems that undermine a marriage.

> *"So they [husband and wife] are no longer two, but one flesh. What therefore God has joined together, let no man separate."* —MATTHEW 19:6

"If you want your marriage to thrive, make sure no other relationship competes with it."

—Robert Lewis

(C) The key is in how we handle those important relationships as a couple.

1. Our spouse must always be our _____ priority.
2. Other relationships must be handled with wisdom and with _____.

II In-laws and Your Marriage

"For this reason a man shall leave his father and his mother, and be joined to his wife; and they shall become one flesh."
—GENESIS 2:24

(A) The joy of extended family

(B) The importance of "leave and cleave"

(C) What to do when you have intrusive or controlling in-laws:

1. Agree as a couple on the _____ that need to be drawn. These boundaries help create proper expectations.

   ▶ Time

   ▶ Money

   ▶ Words

   ▶ Home

   ▶ Holidays

2. These boundaries need to be _____.

3. These boundaries need clear _____ if violated.

   A boundary without consequences is just a suggestion.

4. The _____ should take the lead in communicating these boundaries and enforcing them.

> *"When boundaries are not established in the beginning of a marriage, or when they break down, marriages break down as well. Or such marriages don't grow past the initial attraction and transform into real intimacy ... For this intimacy to develop and grow, there must be boundaries."*[1]
>
> **—Drs. Cloud & Townsend**

III   Children and Your Marriage

"Behold, children are a gift of the LORD; the fruit of the womb is a reward." —PSALM 127:3

We recognize that there are many couples who are struggling with infertility or the loss of a child. Please know that our hearts go out to you. We seek only to encourage you on your journey—whether for healing or in continuing to find a way to bring your own child into the world, adopt, or simply invest in the next generation. God is not only the Giver of Life but our Helper and Sustainer during difficult times.

(A)   Children can bless a marriage in countless ways:

    1.   **They can bring unbelievable joy.**

"I have no greater joy than this, to hear of my children walking in the truth." —3 JOHN 4

    2.   **Children literally express you both in "one flesh."**

(B)   Children can also _____ a marriage.

    1.   **Certain seasons of child rearing are more stressful than others.**

    2.   **Beware the big "W."**

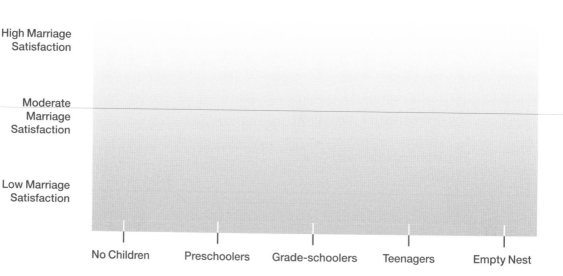

**Preschoolers are physically exhausting.
Teenagers are emotionally exhausting.**

(C)   Children grow up best in the soil of Marriage Oneness.

1.   **Be diligent as husband and wife to _____ and _____ your marriage relationship through all your child-rearing years.**

   ▶   Date weekly without the kids.

   ▶   Get time alone together.

2.   **A healthy marriage is the surest path to having healthy children.**

IV Friends and Your Marriage

"As iron sharpens iron, so one man sharpens another."
—PROVERBS 27:17

(A) Good friends can _____ your Marriage Oneness.

   1. Good friends offer wisdom.

"He who walks with wise men will be wise."
—PROVERBS 13:20

   2. Good friends provide encouragement.

"Therefore encourage one another and build up one another, just as you also are doing." —1 THESSALONIANS 5:11

   3. Good friends motivate you to love and good deeds.

"Let us consider how to stimulate one another to love and good deeds." —HEBREWS 10:24

(B) Choose your friends _____ .

"Man drags man down or man lifts man up."[3]

—Booker T. Washington

"Do not be deceived: 'Bad company corrupts good morals.'"
—1 CORINTHIANS 15:33 (NASB)

V The Priority of Your Marriage

(A) Your marriage relationship should always be your _____ concern.

(B) With healthy boundaries and wise choices, family and friends can greatly benefit your Marriage Oneness.

Jose & Michelle

Q: You two come from very different family backgrounds. How has that impacted your marriage?

Jose: We've figured out how to embrace the differences. My family is very Latino—everybody's always hugging and kissing each other and loud—while her family's more reserved and quiet. But I really liked how her family was so close knit. Coming from a broken home, I wanted that too.

Q: How'd you get there?

Jose: Through a constant series of adjustments. For instance, I had to come to see Michelle's mom as uniquely created and designed by God and find ways to show her honor. And she had to figure out my sense of humor.

Michelle: We established early in our marriage that we were a family of our own, and that our extended family was not going to dictate what we did on holidays or anything else. Establishing those parameters—that it was up to us, not them—really relieved a lot of tension for me in trying to make everyone happy.

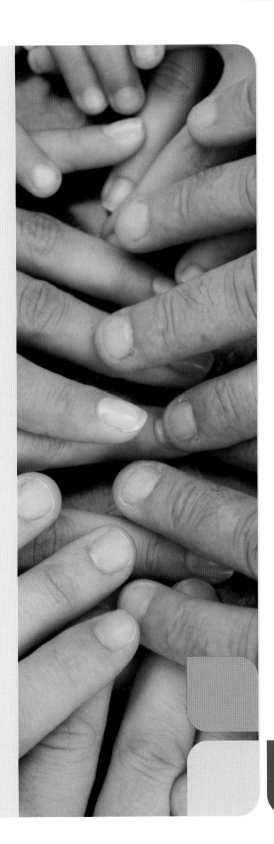

circle**up** ...

Congratulations! You're now at the finish line of this *Marriage Oneness* series! That being the case, take 20 minutes and use the following questions to process this session on family and friends. Then use an additional 10 minutes to complete your final **OnenessWork** assignment.

1.   What was the most important thing you learned in this final session? Explain.

2.   Do you feel your marriage is safe from the interference of in-laws, friends, and children, or did any "red flags" go up during this session about the need for drawing boundaries? If so, what were they?

3. What issue concerns you the most when it comes to family and friends? Explain.

4. Do you have friends around you who are actively seeking to build strong and godly marriages? Who are they and how do they encourage you?

5. What possible **next step** could you take together to further improve your Marriage Oneness in this important area of family and friends? Turn to your **Next Steps Planner** and record your answer.

Oonenesswork

To conclude this ***Marriage Oneness*** series, use your final 10 minutes for deciding what next steps you, as a couple, can begin to pursue together for growing closer together in the weeks ahead.

To do this assignment, each of you should individually look over the **Next Steps Planner** in your workbooks. Review the seven next steps you decided on together during this series as possible future action for building oneness in your marriage.

After doing so, select one next step (only one) you personally want to take in the near future.

Now share your selections with each other, explaining why this particular next step was your preferred choice.

After sharing your selections, make a firm commitment to each other to implement these two next steps (or next step if you chose the same one) in the coming weeks. Do this as a gift to each other for growing closer. We encourage you to formalize this commitment by filling out and signing the **OUR COMMITMENT** pledge (page 129) in each other's workbooks.

successstory

family and friends

Scott & Catherine Mercer

When Scott and Catherine Mercer married twenty-seven years ago, Scott wasn't sure he even wanted to have children. He had grown up in a home wounded by divorce and alcoholism, and he feared that he would pass damaging traits on to his children. But marrying Catherine, who came from a dedicated, large Italian family, gave him hope. Within five years, they had three children.

But Catherine had her own concerns. "In my family," she says, "with five children, my dad worked long hours, and my mother ran a *very* tight ship. There wasn't abuse, like Scott dealt with, but it wasn't easy." She glances at Scott, and he takes her hand. "We knew we wanted to do family life differently than our own parents did."

The Mercers stood against the cultural tide and chose to be a single-income family in a high-income neighborhood. "We knew we wanted something more than we had grown up with," Catherine says, "But that didn't just mean more, financially. A good portion of our income was going toward the mortgage. But in some ways, being limited financially helped us keep things really simple, which is what we wanted. We wanted the kids to have more of us, not more stuff. We fought against getting caught in the web; we didn't enroll the kids in every sport and activity imaginable. We didn't hop on a plane to Disney like everyone else;

we drove to the Jersey shore. We didn't have the newest toys or cars. But what did we have?" she asks, leaning forward. "Dinner together, almost every night."

"Families are so stressed out these days," Scott says. "If your kid is involved in more than one activity and you have two kids, your family is moving in all those directions too. We wanted our direction to be toward one another."

"So we kept it simple as long as we could," Catherine says. "When the kids got older, it was harder, but in the early years, we focused on building a foundation of God and family. Every night at six, we sat down to dinner. We did devotions. We played, prayed, and read lots of books together."

Once the Mercer children hit high school, it became more challenging—the nightly meals, the limitations on activities—but all along, that foundation served them well. "Listen," Catherine says, "even church activities can become demanding. You have to be tough, saying no to even things that *sound* like you should say yes to them. You have to keep the family's greater good in mind."

And how did they handle interactions with extended family—grandparents they didn't always think were living an exemplary life? With respect and grace.

"You know," Scott says, "regardless of where you come from, God asks us to honor our parents. My mom has been married three times. I had to deal with the fact that my dad was an alcoholic and abusive at times. And I don't have to honor bad behavior, but I do need to honor them." That didn't mean he excused their decisions. "But instead of punishing them for past sins, I chose to treat them with a measure of grace just as God does with each of us."

"You can either poison your children over what has happened behind you," Catherine says, "or make a decision to do things differently going forward. Scott never created a monstrous picture of his upbringing—anything our own children would fear. He made sure the kids were safe, and then he did his best to build on the relationship that was there."

"Friends and family can destroy a relationship," Scott says, "or they can be building blocks in the foundation. We elected to make them building blocks. And, by God's grace, this family's legacy *is* different."

suggestedresources

Looking for more information on the subject of family and friends?

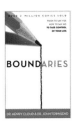

Boundaries
by Dr. Henry Cloud and
Dr. John Townsend
A boundary is a personal property line that marks those things for which we're responsible physically, mentally, emotionally, and spiritually. Boundaries define who we are—and who we're not. Explore how wise boundaries can impact all areas of your life, and enjoy the freedom of a healthy, balanced lifestyle with more fulfilling relationships.

Boundaries in Marriage (small-group series)
by Dr. Henry Cloud and Dr. John Townsend
Only when a husband and wife know and respect each other's needs, choices, and freedom can they give themselves freely and lovingly to one another. By applying the powerful biblical and relational principles presented in this DVD, couples can make a good marriage better—and even save one that's headed for disaster.

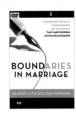

The Smart Stepfamily
by Ron Deal
Discover practical, realistic solutions to the unique spiritual and relational issues stepfamilies face. Through seven effective, achievable steps, you'll move toward building a healthy marriage and a workable peaceful stepfamily.

Raising Kids for True Greatness
by Tim Kimmel
Sometimes greatness is measured by possessions or power. Yet true greatness is an evidence of internal attitudes—a heart known for humility, compassion, graciousness, and enthusiasm. *Raising Kids for True Greatness* exposes the shallow wisdom of the world, giving parents a map to guide children toward rich lives of eternal value and significance.

125

next steps suggestions

Stuck in trying to come up with next steps for your **Next Steps Planner**? Here are some ideas to get you thinking in the right direction:

▶ Apply to our marriage one specific action step recommended in the session.

▶ Read a book together on this subject.

▶ Ask a couple for advice and help with the problem(s) we're having in this area.

▶ Join a small group studying this subject.

▶ Attend a seminar or conference that speaks specifically to this issue.

▶ Watch a video series that goes deeper into this subject.

▶ Get a couple to mentor us in the issues we're struggling with.

▶ Pray together and ask for God's help.

▶ Talk to a pastor.

▶ Go to counseling.

▶ Seek the advice of a specialist or professional in this area.

▶ Take a weekend away to talk together about this.

▶ Recommit to action steps we once did but have stopped doing.

▶ Forgive.

next steps planner

After each session's OnenessWork, record one next step you could take together as a couple to advance oneness in your marriage after this *Marriage Oneness* series is over. To stimulate your thinking, a list of possible next steps is provided on the preceding page.

Session	Oneness Area	Your Next Step ...
2	Communication	
3	Conflict Resolution	
4	Money	
5	Spiritual Beliefs	
6	Sexual Intimacy	
7	Roles & Responsibilities	
8	Family & Friends	

Our Commitment

We commit to pursue greater oneness for our marriage by implementing in the weeks ahead the following next steps as our marriage gifts to each other.

Wife's preferred next step: _____

_____

Husband's preferred next step: _____

_____

_____

WIFE'S SIGNATURE

_____

HUSBAND'S SIGNATURE

Date: _____

What You Now Leave This
Marriage Oneness Series With ...

- A clear **definition** of Marriage Oneness to guide and encourage you:

Marriage Oneness is ...
soul-level harmony of
MIND (common direction),
HEART (emotional connection), and
WILL (mutual commitment)
between a husband and a wife.

- The ***Marriage Oneness Profile*** that objectively measured the level of oneness currently in your marriage. Hopefully, you will take this *Profile* again a year from now and see great improvement. We recommend taking the *Marriage Oneness Profile* on your wedding anniversary each year as a marriage checkup.

- An overview of the **seven key elements** of Marriage Oneness you must grow in for your relationship to be satisfying and long-lasting.

- A number of **OnenessWork** successes that have helped you to go deeper and grow stronger in your marriage.

- Two **Next Steps** for you to take in the weeks ahead to grow your marriage even closer!

Endnotes

Session 1

1. W. Bradford Wilcox and Steven L. Nock, "What's Love Got To Do With It?" *Social Forces: International Journal of Social Research* 84, no. 3 (2006): 1321-1345; Wilcox and Nock, "'Her' Marriage after the Revolutions," *Sociological Forum* 22, no. 1 (March 2007): 103-110.

2. Paul Tournier, *To Understand Each Other* (Louisville, KY: Westminster John Knox Press, 1967), 6.

Session 2

1. George Bernard Shaw, in Marlene Caroselli, *Leadership Skills for Managers* (New York: McGraw-Hill, 2000), 71.

2. Neil Clark Warren, *Learning to Live With the Love of Your Life* (Wheaton, IL: Tyndale House, 1995), 87.

3. Dennis Rainey, *Staying Close* (Dallas: Word, 1989), 203.

4. Gary Chapman, *The Five Love Languages* (Chicago: Northfield, 2010), 10.

Session 3

1. André Maurois, in Tim and Joy Downs, *Fight Fair! Winning at Conflict Without Losing at Love* (Chicago: Moody, 2010), 17.

2. Ellen McCarthy, "Marriage Maintenance," *Arkansas Democrat-Gazette* (Wed., July 14, 2010), E1.

3. Tournier, *To Understand Each Other*, 33.

4. Downs, *Fight Fair!,* 128.

Session 4

1. John Maxwell, in Dave Ramsey, *Total Money Makeover* (Nashville: Thomas Nelson, 2007), 62.

2. Ron Blue, *Master Your Money* (Nashville: Thomas Nelson, 1997), 9.

3. Ibid., 124.

4. Ramsey, *Total Money Makeover*, 5-6.

5. Ramsey, 100.

Session 5

1. Naomi Schaefer Riley, "Love Conquers All: Except Religion," *Arkansas Democrat-Gazette* (Sunday, June 27, 2010), 3H.

2. Ibid.

3. Patrick Morley, *The Man In the Mirror* (Grand Rapids, MI: Zondervan, 1989), 91.

4. Ty Wenger, "5 Things Super-Happy Couples Do Every Day," www.redbookmag.com/love-sex/advice/super-happy-couples-ll-6.

Session 6

1. Dr. Clifford and Joyce Penner, in Dr. Neil Clark Warren, *Learning to Live with the Love of Your Life* (Wheaton: Tyndale, 1995), 123.

2. Warren, *Learning to Live with the Love of Your Life*, 131.

3. Kevin Leman, *7 Things He'll Never Tell You: But You Need to Know* (Nashville: Tyndale House, 2007), 103.

4. Karen Linamen, *Pillow Talk* (Grand Rapids, MI: Revell, 2004), 27.

Session 7

1. Shaunti Feldhahn, *For Women Only: What You Need to Know About the Inner Lives of Men* (Sisters, OR: Multnomah, 2004), 23.

2. Oriel Sullivan and Scott Coltrane, "USA: Men's Changing Contribution to Housework and Child Care," 11th Annual Conference of the Council on Contemporary Families, (Chicago: University of Illinois, April 25-26, 2008), www.contemporaryfamilies.org/subtemplate.hph?t+briefingPapers& ext+menshousework.

3. Katherine Benenati, "Dividing Up Household Chores Can Be Divisive," *Arkansas Democrat-Gazette* (March 3, 2010), E1.

Session 8

1. Dr. Henry Cloud and Dr. John Townsend, *Boundaries in Marriage* (Grand Rapids, MI: Zondervan, 1999), 169.

2. "Happiness for America's young people often means family ties, faith, belonging," AP/MTV poll by Knowledge Networks, Inc. (August 2007), www.socialtechnologies.com/FileView.aspx?filename=AP1.pdf.

3. Booker T. Washington, 1856-1915, public domain.

LifeReady™ is a biblical strategy for the church that uses lay-led, high-impact video resources to provide success training for today's marriages and families.

Research shows that the majority of our happiness in life flows from two primary relationships: with our spouse and with our children. The stronger and better these relationships are, the more satisfying and fulfilling are our lives. The more couples—especially young couples—who can be prepared beforehand and trained in biblically sound marriage-and-family skills, the greater the opportunity they have for success.

Good marriages and families don't just happen; they must be intentionally built. This is the passion behind LifeReady. Each LifeReady resource is more than a study or a visual experience to enjoy. LifeReady is about life-changing training that enables couples to improve their performance while developing new skills and practices.

This does not mean that the LifeReady experience will be dry. On the contrary, each resource is designed to be visually compelling, highly engaging, enjoyable, and fun. But training is at the heart of it all. That's because training is essential to success in life. And success training for today's marriages and families is what LifeReady is all about.